Multimodal Affective Computing: Affective Information Representation, Modelling, and Analysis

Authored By

Gyanendra K. Verma
Department of Information Technology, National Institute of Technology Raipur,
Chhattisgarh, India

Multimodal Affective Computing:
Affective Information Representation, Modelling, and Analysis

Author: Gyanendra K. Verma

ISBN (Online): 978-981-5124-45-3

ISBN (Print): 978-981-5124-46-0

ISBN (Paperback): 978-981-5124-47-7

First published in 2023.

Bentham Science Publishers Pte. Ltd.
80 Robinson Road #02-00
Singapore 068898
Singapore
Email: subscriptions@benthamscience.net

CONTENTS

FOREWORD

Affective Computing is a new area aiming to create intelligent computers that recognize, understand, and process human emotions. Affective Computing is an interdisciplinary area that encompasses a variety of disciplines, such as computer science, psychology, and cognitive science, among others. Emotion may be communicated in various ways, including gestures, postures, and facial expressions, as well as physiological signs, including brain activity, heart rate, muscle activity, blood pressure, and skin temperature. Humans can perceive emotion through facial expressions in general. However, not all emotions, particularly complex ones such as pride, love, mellowness, and sorrow, can be identified only through facial expressions. Physiological signals can therefore be utilized to represent complex emotions effectively.

This book aims to provide the audience with a basic understanding of Affective Computing and its application in many research fields. This state-of-the-art review of existing emotion theory and modeling approaches will help the readers explore various aspects of Affective Computing. By the end of the book, I hope that the readers will be able to understand emotion recognition methods based on audio, video, and physiological signals. Moreover, they will learn the fusion framework and familiarity to implement for emotion recognition.

Shitala Prasad
Institute for Infocomm Research
A*Star
Singapore

PREFACE

Affective Computing is an emerging field with the prime focus on developing intelligent systems that can perceive, interpret, process human emotions and act accordingly. Affective Computing incorporates interdisciplinary research areas like Computer Science, Psychology, Cognitive Science, Machine Learning, *etc*. Machines must perceive and interpret emotions in real-time and act accordingly for intelligent communication with human beings. Emotion plays a significant role in communication and can be expressed through many ways, like facial or auditory expression, gesture or sign language, *etc*. Brain activity, heart rate, muscular activity, blood pressure, and skin temperature are a few examples of physiological signals. It plays a crucial role in affect recognition compared to other emotion modalities. Humans perceive emotion primarily through facial expressions; yet, complex emotions such as pride, love, mellowness, and sorrow cannot be identified just by facial expressions. Physiological signals can thus be employed to recognize complex emotions.

The objective of this book is mainly three-fold: (1) Provide in-depth knowledge about affective Computing, affect information representation, models, and theories of emotions. (2) Emotion recognition from different affective modalities, such as audio, facial expression, and physiological signals, and (2) Multimodal fusion framework for emotion recognition in three-dimensional Valence, Arousal, and Dominance space.

Human emotions can be captured from various modalities, such as speech, facial expressions, physiological signals, *etc*. These modalities provide critical information that may be utilised to infer a user's emotional state. The primary emotions can be captured easily by facial and vocal expressions. However, facial expressions or audio information cannot detect complex emotions. Therefore, an efficient emotion model is required to predict complex emotions. The dimensional model of emotion can effectively model and recognize complex emotions.

Most emotion recognition work is based on facial and vocal expressions. However, the existing literature completely lacks emotion modeling in a continuous space. This book contributes in this direction by proposing an emotion model to predict a large number (more than fifteen) of complex emotions in a three-dimensional continuous space. We have implemented various systems to recognize emotion from speech, facial expression, physiological signals, and multimodal fusion of the above modalities. Our emphasis is on emotion modeling in a continuous space. Emotion prediction from physiological signals as complex emotions is better captured by physiological signals rather than facial or vocal expressions. The main contributions of this book can be summarized as follows:

1. This book presents a state-of-the-art review of Affective Computing and its application in various areas like gaming, medicine, virtual reality, *etc*.
2. A detailed review of multimodal fusion techniques is presented to assimilate multiple modalities to accomplish multimodal fusion tasks. The fusion methods are provided from the perspective of the requirement of multimodal fusions, the level of information fusion, and their applications in various domains, as reported in the literature. Moreover, significant challenges in multimodal fusions are also highlighted. Further, we present the evaluation measures for evaluating multimodal fusion techniques.
3. The significant contribution of this book is the three-dimensional emotion model based on valence, arousal, and dominance. The emotion prediction in three-dimensional space based on valence, arousal, and dominance is also presented.

CONSENT FOR PUBLICATION

Not applicable.

CONFLICT OF INTEREST

The author declares no conflict of interest, financial or otherwise.

Gyanendra K. Verma
Department of Information Technology
National Institute of Technology Raipur
Chhattisgarh
India

ACKNOWLEDGEMENTS

I acknowledge the guidance of Prof. U. S. Tiwary, IIIT Allahabad India, who motivated me to choose Affective Computing as a research topic many years ago. Some of his insights are still present in this book. I want to thank Dr. Shitala Prasad, Scientist, Institute for Infocomm Research, A*Star, Singapore, for his valuable suggestions. And last but not least, Ms. Humaira Hashmi, Editorial Manager Publications, Bentham Books, for extending her kind cooperation to complete this book project.

CHAPTER 1

Affective Computing

Abstract: With the invention of high-power computing systems, machines are expected to show intelligence at par with human beings. A machine must be able to analyze and interpret emotions to demonstrate intelligent behavior. Affective computing not only helps computers to improve performance intelligently but also helps in decision-making. This chapter introduces affective computing and related issues that influence emotions. This study also provides an overview of human-computer interaction (HCI) and the possible use of different modalities for HCI. Further, challenges in affective computing are also discussed, along with the application of affective computing in various areas.

Keywords: Arousal, DEAP database, Dominance, EEG, Multiresolution analysis, Support vector machine, Valence.

1.1. INTRODUCTION

The cognitive, affective, and emotional information is crucial in HCI to improve user-computer connection [1]. It significantly enhances the learning environment. Emotion recognition is crucial since it has several applications in HCI and Human-Robot Interaction (HRI) [2] and many other new fields. Affective computing is a hot topic in the field of human-computer interaction. "Affective Computing is the research and development of systems and technologies that can identify, understand, process, and imitate human emotions," according to the definition.

Affective computing is an interdisciplinary area that encompasses a variety of disciplines, such as computer science, psychology, and cognitive science, among others. Emotions can be exhibited in various ways, such as gestures, postures, facial expressions, and physiological signs, including brain activity, heart rate, muscular activity, blood pressure, and skin temperature [1].

People generally perceive emotion through facial expressions; nevertheless, complex emotions such as pride, gorgeousness, mellowness, and sadness cannot be identified through facial expressions [3]. Physiological signals can therefore be utilized to represent complicated effects.

Gyanendra K. Verma

1.2. WHAT IS EMOTION?

"Everyone knows what an emotion is until asked to give a definition." [4].

Although emotion is prevalent in human communication, the term has no universally agreed meaning. Kleinginna and Kleinginna [5], on the other hand, gave the following definition of emotion:

"Emotion is a complex set of interactions between subjective and objective factors mediated by neural/hormonal systems that can:

1. Generate compelling experiences such as feelings of arousal, pleasure/ displeasure;

2. Generate cognitive processes such as emotionally relevant perceptual effects, appraisals, and labeling processes;

3. Activate widespread physiological adjustments to arousing conditions; and

4. Lead to behavior that is often, but not always, expressive."

1.2.1. Affective Human-Computer Interaction

The researchers described two ways to analyze emotion. The first method divides emotions into joy, fun, love, surprise, grief, *etc*. Another option is to display emotion on a multidimensional or continuous scale. Valence, arousal, and dominance are the three most prevalent aspects. How does a valence scale determine how happy or sad a person is? The arousal scale assesses how relaxed, bored, aroused, or thrilled [6]. The dominance scale depicts submissive (in control) or dominant (empowered) behavior. Emotion identification from facial expressions and voice signals is part of affective HCI. As a result, we will concentrate on the first two modalities, particularly concerning emotion perception. One of the essential needs of MMHCI is that multisensory data be processed individually before being merged.

A multi-modal system may be used in case of insufficient or noisy data. The system may use complementary information from other modalities if one modality's information is absent. If one modality fails to make a decision, the other must do so. Multi-modal HCI (MMHCI) incorporates several domains, such as Artificial Intelligence, Computer Vision, Psychology and others, according to Jaimes A. *et al.* [7]. People communicate frequently using facial expressions, bodily movement, sign language, and other non-verbal communication techniques [8].

Audio and video modalities are commonly employed in man-machine interaction; hence they are vital for HCI. At the feature or choice level, MMHCI focuses on merging several modalities of emotion. Probabilistic graphical models such as the Hidden Markov Model (HMM) and Bayesian Networks are beneficial, according to the study [9]. As a result of its ability to deal with missing values *via* probabilistic inference, Bayesian networks are widely used for data fusion. Vision methods are another option that may be employed for MMHCI [9]. The vision techniques categorize using a human-centered approach and decide how people may engage with the system.

1.3. BACKGROUND

Most emotion recognition research focuses on facial expression and voice emotion [10, 11, 12, 13]. Our book contributed to this approach by presenting an emotion model to predict many complicated emotions in a three-dimensional continuous space, lacking in the previous literature [14]. Even though we have created systems that identify emotion from speech, facial expression, physiological data, and multi-modal fusion of the modalities mentioned above, we focus on emotion modeling in a continuous space and emotion prediction using multi-modal cues.

People usually gather information from various sensory modalities, such as vision (sight), audition (hearing), tactile stimulation (touch), olfaction (smell), and gustation (taste). Then, this information is processed by integrating it into a single cohesive stream of information to communicate with others. In order to integrate numerous complementary and supplemental information, the human brain receives information from multiple communication modalities (such as reading text).

Multi-modal information fusion can be employed in effective systems to integrate related information from different modalities/cues to improve performance [15] and decrease ambiguity in decision-making by reducing data categorization uncertainty. Multi-modal information fusion is necessary for many applications where information from a single modality is inadequate and may contain noise or be insufficient to make conclusions. Consider a visual surveillance system where an object is monitored using visual information. If the object gets occluded, the surveillance system will have no way of tracking it.

Consider a surveillance system that takes information from two modalities (audio and visual information). The object can be tracked even if one of the modalities is unavailable; the system can process the information obtained from other modalities.

The main goal of multi-modal fusion is to combine information from numerous sources in a complementary way to improve the system's performance. This book also looked into multi-modal emotion recognition, an active research topic in Affective Computing. Although emotion identification has been a study topic for decades, the focus has changed from primary emotion to complicated emotion in recent years. Ekman's discrete model of emotion may reflect basic emotions [16].

On the other hand, complex emotions may be described using a dimensional model of emotion since they are multidimensional [17]. This book highlights affective computing and related areas, particularly emotion modeling in three-dimensional continuous space. In subsequent chapters, emotion recognition from physiological signals in three-dimensional space using a benchmark database is also discussed. There are a plethora of survey studies on automated emotion identification [11, 18 - 20], but none focus on a dimensional approach to emotion. As face expressions and voice data cannot identify complicated emotions, physiological signals are the only way to record them.

Furthermore, users can pose or cover their facial emotions. However, they cannot purposefully produce physiological signals since physiological activities are regulated by the central nervous system [21]. As a result, physiological measurements are employed to determine a user's emotional state.

1.4. THE ROLE OF EMOTIONS IN DECISION MAKING

It is vital to comprehend the three fundamental components of emotion properly.

Each part may influence the function and goal of emotional responses.

- Subjective component: How someone feels about it.
- Physiological aspect: How a body responds to the emotion.
- The expressive component is how one can react to the feeling.

According to research, fear raises risk perceptions, disgust increases the likelihood of individuals discarding their items, and pleasure or rage drives people to take action. Emotions have a significant role in decisions, from what one should eat to whom one should vote in elections.

Emotional intelligence, the capacity to recognize and control emotions, has been linked to better decision-making. Research proves that a person with brain injury may be less able to experience emotion and make decisions. Emotions significantly impact even when one feels his decisions are solely based on logic and rationality [22].

1.5. CHALLENGES IN AFFECTIVE COMPUTING

Emotion identification is one of the most recent issues in intelligent human-computer interaction. Most emotion recognition research independently focuses on extracting emotions from visual or aural data. Human beings consider voice and facial emotions the essential indicators during communication. As a result, researchers began to contribute to advancing voice processing and computer vision techniques, among other things. However, there has been a significant increase in Multimodal Human-Computer Interaction (HCI) research due to advancements in hardware technology (low-cost cameras and sensors) [7].

HCI is a multi-disciplinary discipline that includes computer vision, psychology, artificial intelligence, and many other study fields. Explicit commands do not usually interact with new apps and frequently include many users. The advancements in computer processing speed, memory, and storage capacities, along with the availability of a plethora of new input and output devices, have made ubiquitous computing a reality. Phones, embedded systems, PDAs, laptops, wall-mounted screens, and other devices are examples of devices. Due to the enormous variety of computing devices accessible, each with its processing capacity and input/output capabilities, the future of computing will likely involve unique forms of interaction. In order to communicate effectively, input devices must be coordinated, as in human-to-human communication, gestures, speech, haptics, and eye blink all work together [7].

Several studies in facial expression analysis have been published. The major ones are [11, 23 - 27], gesture recognition [28, 29], human motion analysis, and emotion recognition from physiological data [30, 31]. Human emotion recognition has recently been expanded from six fundamental emotions to complex affect recognition in two or three-dimensional (valence, arousal, and dominance) space. It is simple to categorize emotions into distinct groups; however, it is more challenging to categorize complicated emotions. The following are the primary issues in emotion recognition:

1.5.1. How Can Many Emotions Be Analyzed in a Single Framework?

Most emotion recognition research is confined to six or fewer fundamental emotions; however, no emotion framework exists that can examine a wide variety of emotions. Existing emotion research lacks methodologies and frameworks for analyzing many emotions in a single framework.

1.5.2. How Can Complex Emotions Be Represented in a Single Framework Or Model?

Basic emotions (joy, fear, anger, contempt, sorrow, and surprise) are easily identified using a variety of modalities, such as facial expressions, speech, and physiological responses. However, assessing complex emotions (pride, shame, love, melancholy, *etc.*) remains difficult in emotion identification. Complex emotions are challenging to detect since they cannot be represented by facial expressions [32]. We can tell if someone is happy or sad, but measuring little amounts of happiness or sadness is challenging. People frequently express mixed (more than one emotion) or complicated emotions rather than a single emotion, which differs from person to person. Furthermore, because we only have datasets for single emotions, it is difficult to train the system with complicated emotions.

1.5.3. Is The Chosen Theoretical Viewpoint Relevant to other Areas Of Affective Computing?

What additional elements of emotional computing do the chosen theoretical approach and representation apply to? (*e.g.*, if your focus is on recognition, how your representation might extend to emotion modeling. If the focus is emotion generation, how applicable representation would be for modeling emotional effects across multiple modalities).

1.5.4. How Can Physiological Signals Be Used to Anticipate Complicated Emotions?

The human body continually emits physiological signals, such as Electroencephalogram (EEG), Electromyogram (EMG), Respiratory volume (RV), Skin Temperature (SKT), Skin Conductance (SKC), Blood Volume Pulse (BVP), and Heart Rate (HR).

Physiological signals are particularly susceptible to motion artifacts; it is challenging to uniquely map physiological patterns to distinct emotion types [33]. Predicting complicated emotions from physiological markers is also a current research challenge in emotion identification.

1.6. AFFECTIVE COMPUTING IN PRACTICE

Affective computing refers to systems that recognize, analyze, process, and simulate human emotions. The applications/areas where emotion may play a significant role in human-machine communication are listed below:

1.6.1. Avatars or Virtual Agents

With the help of more complicated computer models, recent advancements in computer technology and research have made it possible to mimic genuine social interaction. Virtual agents may now support affective interactions with users that mimic the human appearance and expressive behaviors. Psychiatry and social neurosciences are two intimately interwoven domains of research that have already benefited from virtual agents and affective computing advancements. Indeed, these methodologies balance reproducibility and ecological validity when constructing paradigms that address complicated topics like human interaction, inter-subjectivity, or social behavior.

Virtual reality might help researchers in social neuroscience, requiring realistic yet repeatable experimental scenarios of growing complexity. Many studies in recent years have provided light on contextual influences that may alter social judgments/interactions and the diseases that accompany them. Despite the apparent promise for psychological research, no consensus on experimental procedures in virtual interfaces has yet been achieved. Traditional designs are difficult to rely on because experimental paradigms include nearly limitless degrees of flexibility. Indeed, in interactive environments, the unexpected and chaotic dynamics that occur from many agent interactions must be considered [34].

For the therapeutic use of virtual agents, its real benefit is the ability to simulate interactive social settings without the dangerous or upsetting effects that circumstances have in the actual world. For example, cognitive rehabilitation is already being studied in immersive virtual settings with schizophrenic and autistic subjects. Theoretical insights and experimental data appear to be required to address efficacy, acceptability, and motivation concerns and better incorporate these innovations into integrated remedial programs.

1.6.2. Robotics

Today's researchers attempt to create intelligent robots that can feel, understand, and behave in response to a user's emotional condition. Several research organizations are developing robots that can convey facial emotions. An effective chatbot or robot is an intelligent machine that can communicate with a human being by acquiring, analyzing, and interpreting information and acting intelligently at par with the human being. A chatbot can make decisions and simulate effective responses utilizing effective technologies. In the actual world for a robot or the virtual world for a synthetic character, such an artifact contains different AI modules to build perceptive, decision-making, and reacting capabilities [35].

Affective robots and chatbots add a new level to engagement and have the potential to influence people. Unless a creator has designed the robot to replicate an emotional state, it can do a challenging task and not be proud of it. A robot is a complicated machine that may mimic cognitive capacities. However, it lacks human sentiments and the desire or "appetite for life" that Spinoza refers to as conatus (an effort to persist in existence), encompassing everything from the intellect to the body. Attempts to develop intelligent computers frequently view intelligence as the capacity to fulfill objectives, leaving a critical issue unanswered: whose goals?

The robotics community develops affective computing robots to build a lifetime relationship between a human and an item. Examples of how robots interact with people include allowing autistic children to socialize, assisting youngsters at school, encouraging patients to take prescriptions, and safeguarding the elderly inside a live setting. Their seemingly limitless potential arises partly because it can be physically instantiated, unlike many other technologies.

Social robots will share our environment, live with us in our houses, assist us in our job and daily lives, and even tell us a narrative. Why not make them laugh with some machine humor? Humor is essential in social connections because it reduces stress, boosts confidence, and fosters cooperation. If someone is lonely and miserable, the robot can make them laugh; if someone is furious, it can help put things in perspective by telling them that things are not that awful. If it makes a mistake and knows it, it may be self-deprecating.

1.6.3. Gaming

In gaming, many innovative interfaces are necessary for creating multi-player games. A large number of users interact with one another through novel interfaces. Games are enjoyable to play, and as a result, many people like them. There are various games to choose from and an extensive range of genres.

Games contain the above characteristics; they can impact the player's emotional state, making them useful for teaching and evoking emotions naturally and ethically. It is known as emotional computing in the context of computer games. "Computing that connects to emerges from, or actively impacts emotion," according to Picard [36]. As a result of the wide range of options available when creating games, computer games are an effective instrument for eliciting emotions. Games can be constructed to automatically adjust to the player at run-time, as an illustration of these possibilities.

In gaming and emotions, there are now many studies being done. The majority of studies, however, have included adult subjects. As a result, it would be fascinating to perform our research with young children to see how they connect and express themselves while playing emotional games. Computer games may be utilized to create a pleasant atmosphere and evoke emotions. Combining these components and employing games entertainingly and ethically is intriguing. Knowing this, we would like to look at the impact of emotional games on the mood of Dutch youngsters and determine whether there is a gender difference.

1.6.4. Education

As more open courses become available online, online education is becoming more popular. Using the relationship between effect and cognition to increase learning is a superior concept. Scholars are increasingly concerned about the absence of emotional contact in distant education. They have experimented with a variety of alternatives. *Via* network and multimedia technologies to build a virtual teaching environment; establish a collaborative learning mode; communicate using interactive video and streaming media technology.

These tactics can help mitigate the loss of emotional communication in distance learning to some level. However, they cannot precisely provide emotional encouragement or emotional strategies that correlate to the emotional conditions of the learners. As a result, it cannot assist learners in solving the problem of a lack of feeling. This problem may be effectively solved when affective computing is used in online education. Distance learners arrange emotional information through a sophisticated process. In general, physiological and psychological methods can be used to acquire and assess emotion.

In Emotional information processing and affective computing technologies, physiological measurements are primarily used to get emotional information. The questionnaire method, adjective checklist technique, and projective test method, collectively known as the subjective experience measurement, are examples of psychological measurement. The questionnaire, for example, evaluates the current emotional state and psychological emotions.

1.6.5. Medical

The affective design has produced many applications for phobias, such as fear of flying and fear of heights. Affect-based stress reduction is effective. Several researchers have been experimenting with sensors and algorithms to service various areas of healthcare and improve the lives of patients suffering from stress and depression. DeepAffex [37] has developed an Affective Intelligence platform to measure physiological elements related to well-being, including heart rate, breathing rate, and blood pressure, by just videoing a patient's face. The system is based on facial blood flow imaging. The analytics can be applied to support healthcare by recording videos to see how stressed a subject may have been during a particular experience, such as an interview.

1.6.6. Smart Homes and Workplace Environments

An intelligent house is outfitted with mechanical appliances that react to the user's emotional condition. The user's emotional state influences the lighting settings and music played.

CONCLUSION

This chapter provides the fundamentals of Affective Computing, the definition of emotions, and the role of emotion in decision-making. This chapter also throws light on current challenges associated with Affective Computing. The last application of affective computing is discussed in various fields, including medicine, robotics, smart homes, gaming, education, *etc*.

REFERENCES

[1] K. Schaaff, EEG-based emotion recognition, Ph.D. thesis, Universitat Karlsruhe (TH), 2008.

[2] R. Cowie, E. Douglas-Cowie, N. Tsapatsoulis, G. Votsis, S. Kollias, W. Fellenz, and J.G. Taylor, "Emotion recognition in human-computer interaction", *IEEE Signal Process. Mag.,* vol. 18, no. 1, pp. 32-80, 2001.
[http://dx.doi.org/10.1109/79.911197]

[3] P. Ekman, W.V. Friesen, M. O'Sullivan, A. Chan, I. Diacoyanni-Tarlatzis, K. Heider, R. Krause, W.A. LeCompte, T. Pitcairn, P.E. Ricci-Bitti, K. Scherer, M. Tomita, and A. Tzavaras, "Universals and cultural differences in the judgments of facial expressions of emotion", *J. Pers. Soc. Psychol.,* vol. 53, no. 4, pp. 712-717, 1987.
[http://dx.doi.org/10.1037/0022-3514.53.4.712] [PMID: 3681648]

[4] Beverley Fehr, and James A. Russell, "Concept of emotion viewed from a prototype perspective", *J. Exp. Psychol,* vol. 113.3, p. 464, 1984.
[http://dx.doi.org/10.1037/0096-3445.113.3.464]

[5] P.R. Kleinginna Jr, and A.M. Kleinginna, "A categorized list of emotion definitions, with suggestions for a consensual definition", *Motiv. Emot.,* vol. 5, no. 4, pp. 345-379, 1981.
[http://dx.doi.org/10.1007/BF00992553]

[6] S. Koelstra, A. Yazdani, M. Soleymani, and C. Mü, "Single trial classification of EEG and peripheral physiological signals for recognition of emotions induced by music videos", *Proc. Brain Informatics,* pp. 89-100, 2010.

[7] A. Jaimes, and N. Sebe, "Multimodal human-computer interaction: a survey", *Computer Vision and Image Understanding,* vol. 108, pp. 116-134, 2007.

[8] G.K. Verma, and B.K. Singh, "Facial emotion recognition in curvelet domain", *Commun. Comput. Inf.*

Sci., vol. 157, pp. 554-559, 2011. b
[http://dx.doi.org/10.1007/978-3-642-22786-8_70]

[9] N. Sebe, I. Cohen, A. Garg, and T.S. Huang, *Machine Learning in Computer Vision.* Springer: Berlin, NY, 2005. a

[10] Y.V. Venkatesh, A.A. Kassim, J. Yuan, and T.D. Nguyen, "On the simultaneous recognition of identity and expression from BU-3DFE datasets", *Pattern Recognit. Lett.,* vol. 33, no. 13, pp. 1785-1793, 2012.
[http://dx.doi.org/10.1016/j.patrec.2012.05.015]

[11] M. El Ayadi, M.S. Kamel, and F. Karray, "Survey on speech emotion recognition: Features, classification schemes, and databases", *Pattern Recognit.,* vol. 44, no. 3, pp. 572-587, 2011.
[http://dx.doi.org/10.1016/j.patcog.2010.09.020]

[12] Y.H. Yang, Y.C. Lin, Y.F. Su, and H.H. Chen, "A regression approach to music emotion recognition", *IEEE Trans. Audio Speech Lang. Process.,* vol. 16, no. 2, pp. 448-457, 2008.
[http://dx.doi.org/10.1109/TASL.2007.911513]

[13] Y. Rahulamathavan, R.C.W. Phan, J.A. Chambers, and D.J. Parish, "Facial expression recognition in the encrypted domain based on local fisher discriminant analysis", *IEEE Trans. Affect. Comput.,* vol. 4, no. 1, pp. 83-92, 2013.
[http://dx.doi.org/10.1109/T-AFFC.2012.33]

[14] J. Broekens, "Modeling the experience of emotion", *Int. J. Synth. Emotions,* vol. 1, no. 1, pp. 1-17, 2010. [IJSE].
[http://dx.doi.org/10.4018/jse.2010101601]

[15] J.F. Aguilar, J.O. Garcia, D.G. Romero, and J.G. Rodriguez, "A comparative evaluation of fusion strategies for multimodal biometric verification", *Int. Conf. on Video-Based Biometric Person Authentication VBPA 2003,* 2003pp. 830-837

[16] P. Ekman, R. Levenson, and W. Friesen, "Automatic nervous system activity distinguishes between emotions", *Science,* vol. 221, no. 1, pp. 210-1208, 1983.

[17] P.J. Lang, "The emotion probe: Studies of motivation and attention", *Am. Psychol.,* vol. 50, no. 5, pp. 372-385, 1995.
[http://dx.doi.org/10.1037/0003-066X.50.5.372] [PMID: 7762889]

[18] H. Gunes, and M. Piccardi, "From mono-modal to multi-modal: Affect recognition using visual modalities", ", In: *Ambient intelligence techniques and applications,* D. Monekosso, P. Remagnino, Y. Kuno, Eds., Springer-Verlag: Berlin, Germany, 2008, pp. 154-182.

[19] Zhihong Zeng, M. Pantic, G.I. Roisman, and T.S. Huang, "A survey of affect recognition methods: audio, visual, and spontaneous expressions", *IEEE Trans. Pattern Anal. Mach. Intell.,* vol. 31, no. 1, pp. 39-58, 2009.
[http://dx.doi.org/10.1109/TPAMI.2008.52] [PMID: 19029545]

[20] H. Gunes, M. Piccardi, and M. Pantic, "From the lab to the real world: Affect recognition using multiple cues and modalities", In: *Affective computing, focus on emotion expression, synbook and recognition*Vienna, Austria, 2008, pp. 185-218.

[21] W. Wen, G. Liu, N. Cheng, J. Wei, P. Shangguan, and W. Huang, "Emotion Recognition Based on Multi-Variant Correlation of Physiological Signals", *IEEE Trans. Affect. Comput.,* vol. 5, no. 2, pp. 126-140, 2014.
[http://dx.doi.org/10.1109/TAFFC.2014.2327617]

[22] J.S. Lerner, Y. Li, P. Valdesolo, and K.S. Kassam, "Emotion and decision making", *Annu Rev Psychol.,* vol. 66, pp. 799-823, 2015.
[http://dx.doi.org/doi:10.1146/annurev-psych-010213-115043]

[23] M. Pantic, and L.J.M. Rothkrantz, "Facial action recognition for facial expression analysis from static face images", *IEEE Trans. Syst. Man Cybern. B Cybern.,* vol. 34, no. 3, pp. 1449-1461, 2004.

[http://dx.doi.org/10.1109/TSMCB.2004.825931] [PMID: 15484916]

[24] B. Fasel, and J. Luettin, "Automatic facial expression analysis: a survey", *Pattern Recognit.*, vol. 36, no. 1, pp. 259-275, 2003. [http://dx.doi.org/10.1016/S0031-3203(02)00052-3]

[25] Y. Tian, T. Kanade, and J. Cohn, "Facial expression analysis", In: *Handbook of Face Recognition* Springer, 2005, pp. 1424-1445.

[26] S.G. Koolagudi, and K.S. Rao, "Emotion recognition from speech: a review", *Int. J. Speech Technol.*, vol. 15, no. 2, pp. 99-117, 2012. [http://dx.doi.org/10.1007/s10772-011-9125-1]

[27] Y. Kim, E. Schmidt, R. Migneco, B. Morton, P. Richardson, J. Scott, J. Speck, and D. Turnbull, "Music emotion recognition: a state of the art review", *Proceedings of the 11th International Society for Music Information Retrieval Conference,* 2010pp. 255-266

[28] A. Kleinsmith, and N. Bianchi-Berthouze, "Affective body expression perception and recognition: A survey", IEEE Trans. Affective Computing [http://dx.doi.org/10.1109/T-AFFC.2012.16]

[29] M. Karg, A.A. Samadani, R. Gorbet, K. Kuhnlenz, J. Hoey, and D. Kulic, "Body movements for affective expression: A survey of automatic recognition and generation", *IEEE Trans. Affect. Comput.*, vol. 4, no. 4, pp. 341-359, 2013. [http://dx.doi.org/10.1109/T-AFFC.2013.29]

[30] D. Novak, M. Mihelj, and M. Munih, "A survey of methods for data fusion and system adaptation using autonomic nervous system responses in physiological computing", In: *Interacting with computers* Elsevier, 2012.

[31] H. Gunes, and M. Pantic, "Automatic, dimensional and Continuous Emotion recognition", *Int. J. Synth. Emotions,* vol. 1, no. 1, pp. 68-99, 2010. [http://dx.doi.org/10.4018/jse.2010101605]

[32] P. Ekman, "Facial expression and emotion", *American Psychologist,* vol. 48, no. 4, pp. 384-92, 1993. [http://dx.doi.org/10.1037/0003-066X.48.4.384]

[33] J. Wagner, Kim Jonghwa, and E. Andre, "From physiological signals to emotions: implementing and comparing selected methods for feature extraction and classification", *IEEE International Conference on Multimedia and Expo,* 2005

[34] Brunet Gouet, and Eric Oker, *Advances in virtual agents and affective computing for the understanding and remediation of social cognitive disorders.* Expeditio Institutional Repository University of Bogotá Jorge Tadeo Lozano. University of Bogotá Jorge Tadeo Lozano, 2016. Available from: http://hdl.handle.net/20.500.12010/14368

[35] L. Devillers, "Human–robot interactions and affective computing: the ethical implications", In: *Robotics, AI, and Humanity.* Springer: Cham, 2021, pp. 205-211. [http://dx.doi.org/10.1007/978-3-030-54173-6_17]

[36] R.W. Picard, *Affective Computing.* MIT Press, 1997.

[37] "DeepAffex: Affective intelligence engine—developed by the Nuralogix Corporationh", s Available from: https://www.deepaffex.ai/

CHAPTER 2

Affective Information Representation

Abstract: This chapter presents a brief overview of Affective computing and a formal definition of emotion given by various researchers. Human-computer interaction aims to enhance communication between man and machine so that machines can acquire, analyze, interpret and act on par with human beings. At the same time, Affective human-computer interaction focuses on enhancing communication between man and machines using affective information. Moreover, this chapter deals with Human emotional expression and perception through various modalities such as speech, facial expressions, physiological signals, *etc*. It also detailed the overview of Action Units and Techniques for classifying facial expressions as reported in the literature.

Keywords: Action units, Affective computing, Affective HCI, Emotion expression, Facial expression, HCI.

2.1. INTRODUCTION

A review of multimodal emotional information extraction and processing is presented in this chapter. Affective computing may be thought of as an issue of automatic emotion perception for improved human-machine connection. It entails the detection and interpretation of human emotion as well as the prediction of the user's mental state. It also entails the examination of a person's emotional data in order to determine his or her mental state. Facial emotion identification is explored in the chapter, along with the principles of facial expression and emotion modeling. With the system's limitations, facial expression representation is also available.

2.2. AFFECTIVE COMPUTING AND EMOTION

Affective computing is an interdisciplinary area that encompasses a variety of disciplines, such as computer science, psychology, and cognitive science, among others. Emotion may be exhibited in various ways, including gestures, postures, facial expressions, and physiological signs, heart rate, muscular activity, blood pressure , and skin temperature [1].

Gyanendra K. Verma

According to the definition, "Affective Computing is the research and development of systems and technologies that can identify, understand, process, and imitate human emotions".

People generally perceive emotion through facial expressions; nevertheless, complex emotions such as pride, gorgeousness, mellowness, and sadness cannot be identified through facial expressions [2]. Physiological signals can therefore be utilized to represent complicated effects.

2.2.1. Affective Human-Computer Interaction

The researchers described two ways to analyze emotion. The first method divides emotions into categories, such as joy, fun, love, surprise, grief, *etc.* Another option is to display emotion on a multidimensional or continuous scale. Valence, arousal and dominance are the three most prevalent aspects. How does a valence scale determine how happy or sad a person is? The arousal scale assesses how relaxed, bored, aroused, or thrilled you are [3]. The dominance scale depicts submissive (in control) or dominant (empowered) behavior. Emotion identification from facial expressions and voice signals is part of affective HCI. As a result, we will concentrate on the first two modalities, particularly concerning emotion perception. One of the essential needs of MMHCI is that multisensory data be processed individually before being merged.

Multimodal HCI (MMHCI) incorporates several domains, such as Artificial Intelligence, Computer Vision, Psychology, and others, according to Jaimes A. *et al.* [4]. When people connect, they frequently employ both verbal and nonverbal communication. Non-verbal communication includes facial expressions, bodily movement, sign language, and other non-verbal techniques [5].

The most commonly used modalities in HCI are audio and video; hence, they are vital for HCI. Multimodal HCI focuses on merging several modalities of emotion at the feature or decision level. Probabilistic graphical models such as the Hidden Markov Model (HMM) and Bayesian Networks are beneficial, according to [6]. As a result of its ability to deal with missing values, Bayesian networks are commonly utilized for data fusion through probabilistic inference. Vision methods are another option that may be employed for MMHCI [6]. The vision techniques categorize using a human-centered approach and decide how people may engage with the system.

2.2.2. Human Emotion Expression and Perception

"Everyone knows what an emotion is, until asked to give a definition." [7].

Although emotion is prevalent in human communication, the term has no universally agreed meaning. (Kleinginna and Kleinginna) [8].

On the other hand, it gave the following definition of emotion:

1. "Emotion is a complex set of interactions between subjective and objective factors mediated by neural/hormonal systems that can:

2. Generate compelling experiences, such as feelings of arousal, pleasure/displeasure; b) Generate cognitive processes, such as emotionally relevant perceptual effects, appraisals, and labeling processes;

3. Activate widespread physiological adjustments to arousing conditions; and

4. Lead to behavior that is often, but not always, expressive."

Automatic Human Emotion Recognition captures and extracts information from numerous emotional modalities. We have a wide range of sensors and devices to gather voice data, visual signals, linguistic contents, and physiological signals, among other things, in order to capture emotional information. Although emotional information may be expressed in various ways, Fig. (**2.1**) depicts the most commonly utilized signals reported in the literature.

2.2.2.1. Facial Expressions

The majority of the study has focused on detecting emotion through facial expressions. One of the most dependable and natural ways to communicate emotion is through facial expression. We may quickly detect another person's enjoyment, grief, disagreement, and intentions during the conversation by facial expression. Another advantage of facial expression is that anybody may show it, regardless of age or gender. As a result, affective computing's primary source/channel is facial expression.

2.2.2.2. Audio and Speech

For spoken communication, audio is the most common channel. A speech reflects the style of communication by conveying emotion through linguistic and paralinguistic signals. In any event, a person's affective state may be deduced directly from speech. Emotion theory shows that a physiological response accompanies the emotional state. When we are walking through a jungle, we are afraid. We start shaking and sweating as a wild animal arrives abruptly in front of us. This is due to the physiological changes that occur in our bodies. The tone of voice also changes depending on the user's emotional condition. When we are joyful, we speak healthily, and when we are mellow, we speak in a low manner.

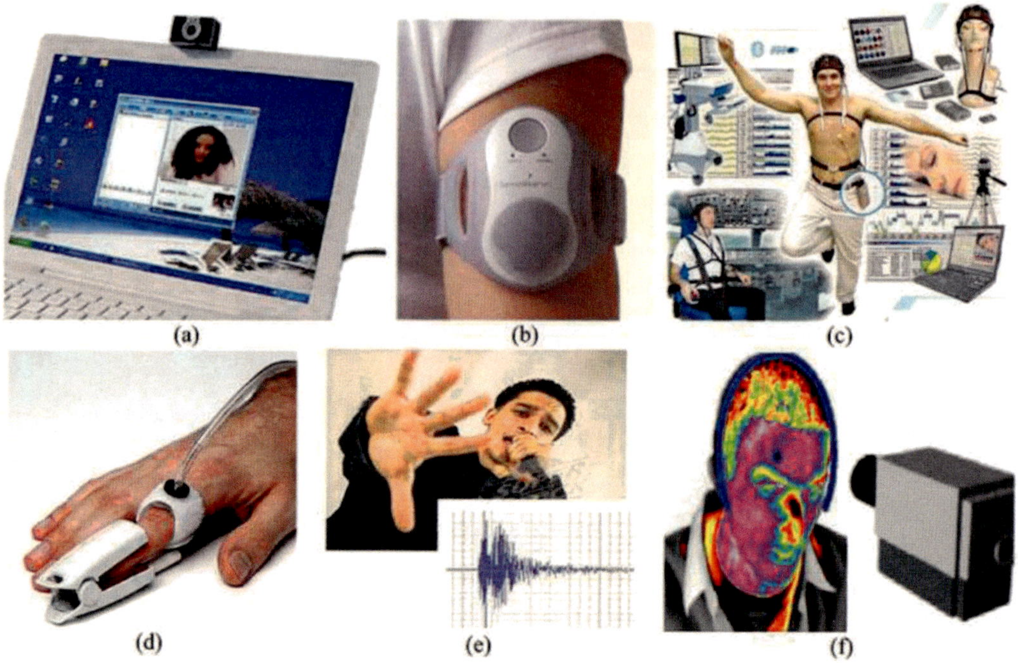

Fig. (2.1). Example of different emotion modalities: **a)** camera **b)** body media sensors **c)** physiological signal recorder **d)** pulse wave signal recorder **e)** Audio recorder **f)** Infrared camera.

2.2.2.3. Physiological Signals

Most emotion theories are based on physiological changes that occur when emotions are evoked. Emotion theory states that as we experience emotions, our bodies undergo physiological changes. According to some studies, emotion is caused by the activation of the autonomic nervous system. The human neurological system directly regulates physiological reactions; they are more resistant to putative products of human social masking [9]. Electroencephalogram (EEG), Electromyogram (EMG), Electrooculogram (EOG), Galvanic Skin Response (GSR), Blood volume pressure, Respiration pattern, Skin temperature, and other modalities make up the physiological signal. Physiological signals include various clues and can be utilized in health, entertainment, and human-computer interaction applications.

Schaaff K. *et al.* [1] discussed the benefits of physiological markers in predicting emotion. The central nervous system regulates bio-signals; they cannot be manipulated purposefully, whereas actors may manipulate their facial expressions. Physiological signals are continuously emitted, and because the sensors are linked to the subject's body, they are never out of reach. Physiological data may be utilized with other emotional data such as voice or facial expression.

Furthermore, physiological patterns aid in assessing and quantifying stress, anger, and other emotions that impact health [6]. One of the disadvantages of employing physiological signals is capturing method. The physiological signals are measured using highly intrusive methods, such as sensors placed on the user's body, which is not ideal for most natural contact.

2.2.2.4. Hand and Gesture Movement

Emotional states have been emphasized in social psychology and human development research [10]. Although several studies have been published on evaluating and annotating physical movement, the intricacy of mapping body gestures to emotional information remains a challenge. Body movement may emphasize and enhance emotional information sent through other channels during communication. For example, after slamming a sharp edge into the table, we communicate our rage with our words and expression.

Emotional body language research has also looked into many elements of emotion displayed through movement, such as how emotions modify different behaviors like walking or knocking. Other studies employed generic nonverbal expressions of emotions. The research topics explored in the linked studies fully justify the utilized settings. Such limits are likely to prohibit actors from expressing emotions; naturally, that would be characteristic of regular human-human interactions [11].

The emotional channels indicated above can be researched separately or combined to incorporate affective information complementary. Multimodal fusion has been successfully used in much research to increase the robustness and accuracy of machine emotion analysis.

2.3. RECOGNITION OF FACIAL EMOTION

Facial expressions are a prime mode to exhibit emotions by human beings and are widely used in day-to-day communication. People make first contact through face during communication with others. As a result, mainstream emotion research has concentrated on facial expressions despite the wide range of indicators and modalities accessible in human-human emotional contact. As a result, most previous research on automated emotion identification has concentrated on facial expressions.

When we are walking through a jungle, we are afraid. We start shaking and sweating as a wild animal arrives abruptly in front of us. The tone of voice changes depending on the user's emotional condition. When we are joyful, we speak healthily, and when we are mellow, we speak in a low manner.

2.3.1. Facial Expression Fundamentals

Besides verbal communication, facial expression is an effective means of nonverbal communication. Under the heading of human-computer interaction, one of the most research-oriented areas is releasing [12] book "The Expressions of the Emotions in Man and Animal", which marks the beginning of facial expression study. Many researchers have been drawn to the study of facial expressions due to this book. According to Darwin, nonverbal communication is "species-specific" but not "culture-specific" according to Darwin. After every occurrence, he added, facial expressions are one type of physiological reaction. The first is the notion of acceptable linked behavior, which Darwin argues is the foundation for developing facial expressions.

Darwin stated in his book that particular complicated activities are direct or indirect functions of some states of mind. Further, whenever the same state of mind is induced, there is an affinity for comparable actions to be undertaken, albeit they may not be of the slightest value. When an opposite straight state of mind is produced, there is a solid and automatic propensity to do activities of a precisely opposite type. One example may be given as the position of a dog's tail or the ears of many other animals; upward when they are brave or expressively hopeful, and down when they are helpless, fearful, or pessimistic by various researchers:

- When a person or animal is not attempting to hide his feelings, his facial expressions betray emotional behavior.
- Animals or people cannot hide their feelings if they are not arranged ahead of time. If emotional deception is efficient but not complete, observers can more accurately anticipate the emotion of species.
- Facial expressions are species-dependent; thus, they might be the same for animals of various races.
- Species that predominantly employ spontaneous facial expressions during communication find it difficult to mask their feelings using set expressions.

As the preceding arguments show, expressiveness is crucial in identifying human behavior. It is also difficult for people to disguise it without prior planning. So the primary issue is determining which phrase corresponds to which activity and correctly recognizing them.

2.3.2. Emotion Modeling

There are three steps to recognizing emotions: i) Emotion modeling ii), Emotion categorization and iii) System evaluation. To model emotion, we must first understand how emotion arises in humans. In order to get the answer to the issue, we must go into cognitive science. According to cognitive science, emotion is an emotional state that arises in humans (animals) reacting to inputs. It entails a series of physiological responses to stimuli or events. It is worth noting that functionalist methods of emotions differ depending on the level of analysis: individual, dyadic (inter-personal between two persons), group, and cultural levels of study.

Emotion can be expressed on social, cultural, or other levels. The group and cultural levels of analysis see emotions as social and cultural functions. They believe individuals or groups in social contexts construct emotions. They link them to individual constructs, social hierarchy patterns, language, or socio-economic organization requirements, among other things [13]. We are primarily concerned with the emotion involved in human interactions [14, 15] are two examples of [14, 15], respectively.

Ekman assigns facial activity units. One of the most prominent visual clues to discern emotion from facial expressions is [16]. A facial action unit (FAU) is responsible for detecting visual information and recognizing automatic effects. In order to adequately capture these facial activity units, a three-dimensional model is required. Ekman and Friesen pioneered Action Units (AUs) to express emotion. They created the Face Action Coding System (FACS) for linguistically coding fine-grained changes in facial appearance to represent the intricacy of human facial action. Facial expression variations are linked to the motions of the muscles that create them, according to FACS. There are 44 separate action movements defined in this document. "Inner section of the brows is elevated" (AU1), "outer portion of the brows is raised" (AU2), and so on are some instances of linguistic descriptions of AUs. Some of the AUs are shown in Fig. (**2.2**).

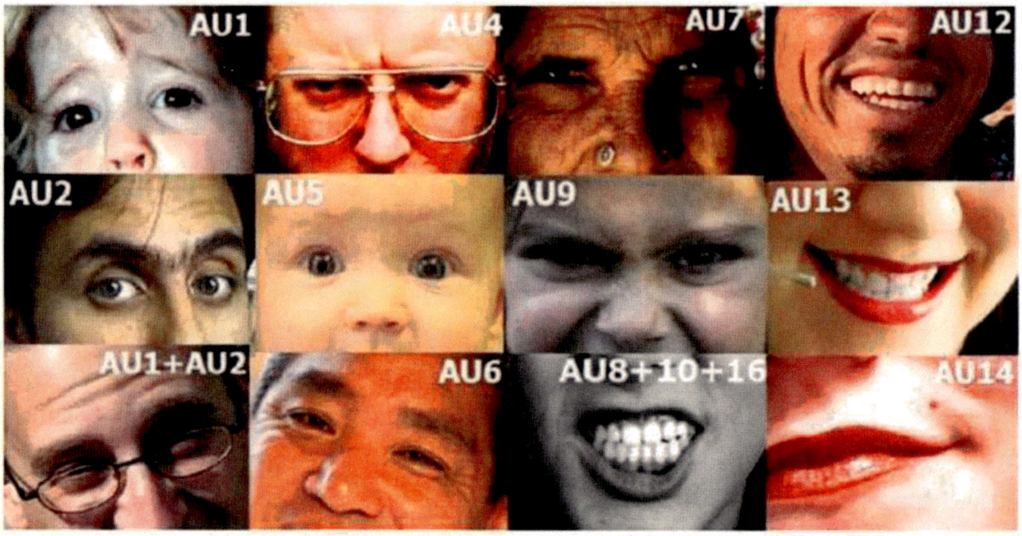

Fig. (2.2). Example action units from Ekman and Friesen's facial action coding method [16].

2.3.3. Representation of Facial Expression

One of the most challenging aspects of facial expression recognition is capturing an expression that expresses a wide range of emotions. The lips, eyes, eyebrows, cheeks, and chin are the critical areas of our body that convey emotional emotions.

Wrinkles and bulges are examples of other facial expressions [17, 18]. As most facial emotions may be seen through other body areas, it is necessary to detect the face and compute the associated attributes alone from the face. The backdrop subtraction approach is another way to remove the background from a facial expression. We can improve the collected face characteristics using filters/algorithms like the Gabor Wavelet-based filter [19, 20]. The improved characteristics are rich in emotional information.

Texture information, which provides information about spatial gradients, is frequently used to portray facial characteristics. Textural characteristics readily represent emotions. The two most important factors that influence system performance are illumination and noise. The illumination is the difference in brightness caused by unequal light reflection from the eyes, teeth, and skin. It is challenging to capture emotional expression in various noise and lighting situations. There are, however, several robust techniques for reducing the effects of light and noise.

2.3.4. Facial Emotion's Limitations

Machine recognition of facial expressions remains difficult in pattern recognition due to environmental changes, real-time processing requirements, such as time and space, and other factors. The issue, as mentioned earlier, has drawn pattern recognition researchers to this topic. Feature selection or extraction for identification, preprocessing, and classification tasks under various conditions are some additional significant problems [21].

The majority of emotion recognition methods are constrained in some way:

- View or posture, location, and orientation of the head relative to the camera.
- Scaling of the head.
- Environmental clutter and illumination.
- Image backdrop complexity.
- Occlusion (partial or complete) and unregulated illumination.
- Gender, disease, age, and other factors can cause facial variation.
- Beards, facial hair, and make-up shaved or grown.
- Deformities of the face.

Scaling, location, and resistance to translation and in-plane rotation are constraints that may be avoided using preprocessing approaches. The most challenging limitation is the out-of-plane rotation of the facial picture, which results in several views of the image. As a result, additional study into posture invariant expression identification is needed. They induce the loss of crucial face characteristics, environmental clutter, illumination, complicated backgrounds, and occlusion, negatively impacting expression detection.

Some authors have developed algorithms for expression recognition under such constraints. However, these constraints cannot be avoided in a real-world setting. As a result, an adaptive expression recognition system that can adapt to changing environmental conditions is required. However, researchers have not paid enough attention to these adaptive mechanisms. The researchers have proposed that auditory and visual facial expression features can be utilized to construct a robust emotion detection system.

2.3.5. Techniques for Classifying Facial Expressions

A classifier must be used with an independent facial model to categorize the user's facial mood. The classifier used to characterize emotion might be linear or non-linear. A linear classifier can be employed for the facial images; however, non-linear or dynamic classifiers are utilized to analyze the emotional information data in time series. In Table **2.1**, a list of several emotion identification systems, along with their accuracy and modality, are depicted.

Table 2.1. Methods, modalities, and accuracy of emotion recognition systems.

Study	Method	Signals	Accuracy
S. Koelstra *et al.* (2013)	PSD Facial action unit	EEG and facial expression	86.7%
S. M. Lajevardi *et al.* (2012)	TPCF	Video	87.05%
M. Soleymony *et al.* (2012)	Electorencaphlogram	Video	76.4%
M. A. Nicolaou *et al.* (2011)	MFCC and feature point	Audio-visual	91.0%
A. Chakraborty *et al.* (2009)	Segmentation	Video	88.0%
Y. Wang *et al.* (2008)	MFCC/ Gabor wavelet	Audio-visual	82.14%
A. Kapoor *et al.* (2007)	Pixel difference in ROC	Video	79.17%
M. Pantic *et al.* (2006)	Facial features	Video	86.3%

Support Vector Machine (SVM), Artificial Neural Network (ANN), Principal Component Analysis (PCA), Fuzzy Logic, Genetic Algorithm, Wavelet Transform, Gabor Transform, Adaboost, The Fisher criteria, Haar Transform, Curvelet Transform, and other approaches are used to identify emotions. PCA is a dimensionality reduction approach that has been widely employed in facial expression recognition [22 - 25]. Several researchers have employed SVM, a state-of-the-art machine learning approach, in their work [26 - 30].

Deep Learning (DL) has achieved the best pattern recognition accuracy in recent years. We are providing a separate table (Table **2.2**) of emotion recognition systems based on DL.

Table 2.2. Methods, modalities, and accuracy of emotion recognition systems based on Deep Learning.

Study	Year	Dl Model	Layers/Strategy	Modality	Emotion States (No. Of Classes)	Accuracy (%)
Wu *et al.* [31]	2022	CNN	3 Convolution layers and 1 fully connected layer.	Physiological Signals	Valence (2), Arousal (2), Dominance (2) and Liking (2)	99.36 (V), 99.37 (A), 99.39 (D), 99.46 (L)

(Table 2.2) cont.....

Study	Year	Dl Model	Layers/Strategy	Modality	Emotion States (No. Of Classes)	Accuracy (%)
Wang *et al* [32]	2022	2D CNN	8 Convolution layers 4 batch normalizations 4 drop-out layers 3 max-pooling layers, 2 fully connected layers	EEG	Valence (2), Arousal (2)	99.98 (V) and 99.9 (A)
Bao *et al* . [33]	2022	CNN	Graph construction block Graph convolutional block Style-based recalibration module Classification block	EEG	Positive (5), Neutral (5) and Negative (5)	95.08
Wang *et al* . [34]	2022	CNN	Normal Cell Reduction cell Temporal Cell	EEG	Happy, Neutral and Sad	92.24
Hu *et al* . [35]	2021	ScalingNet	Multi-kernel convolutional layers Feature extraction Feature Map transform Classification	EEG	Valence (2), Arousal (2), Dominance (2)	DEAP- 71.65 (A), 71.32 (V), 72.89 (D) SEED- 73.89 (A), 69.28 (V)
Zheng *et al* . [36]	2021	CNN	3 Convolutional layers 1 Reconstruction layer 1 Fully connected layer	EEG	Valence (2), Arousal (2)	subject-dependent - 93.61 (V) and 94.04 (A) Subject-independent - 83.83 (V) and 84.53 (A)
Islam *et al* . [37]	2021	CNN	3 Convolution layers 3 ReLU layers 3 Polling Layers	EEG	Valence (2), Arousal (2)	78.22 (V) and 74.92 (A)
Salama *et al* . [38]	2021	3D-CNN	2 convolution layers Max-pooling layer Fully connected layer	EEG	Valence (2), Arousal (2)	96.13 (V), and 96.79 (A)

(Table 2.2) cont.....

Study	Year	Dl Model	Layers/Strategy	Modality	Emotion States (No. Of Classes)	Accuracy (%)
Ganapathy *et al*. [39]	2021	Multiscale CNN	1 Convolution 1 Subsampling or pooling 1 ReLU layer 1 fully connected layer	Electrodermal activity	Valence (2), Arousal (2)	69.33 (V) and 71.43 (A)
Ozdemir *et al*. [40]	2021	Deep CNN	3 Convolution layers 3 max-pool layers 3 ReLU function 1 fully connected layer	EEG	Valence (2), Arousal (2), Dominance (2), Liking (2)	90.62 (V), 86.13 (A), 88.48 (D) and 86.23 (L)
Zhou *et al* [41]	2021	3D CNN	4 Convolution3D blocks 1 Fully connected layer 1 SoftMax layer	EEG	Strong positive, weak positive, neutral, weak negative, and strong negative	98.57
Garg *et al*. [42]	2021	CNN	Convolution 1D and 2D layers Pooling layers fully connected layers SoftMax/logistic layer	EEG	Arousal (2), Valence (2), dominance (2)	96.63 (A), 95.87 (V) and 96.30 (D)
Liu *et al*. [43]	2021	3D Convolution attention neural network	4 layers of 3DCNN structure, 2 Attention mechanism blocks 3 layers are multilayer perceptron blocks	EEG	Positive, Neutral and Negative.	Subject-Independent - 96.37 Subject-Dependent - 97.35
Chen *et al*. [44]	2021	1DCNN	3 Convolutional Layers 2 Batch Normalization Layers 3 Pooling Layers 1 Flatten Layer 5 Fully-Connected Layer	EEG	Valence (2), Arousal (2)	97.47 (V) and 97.76 (A)

(Table 2.2) cont.....

Study	Year	Dl Model	Layers/Strategy	Modality	Emotion States (No. Of Classes)	Accuracy (%)
Hssayeni *et al*. [45]	2021	CNN	3 Convolutional blocks 2 Fully connected layers	Physiological Signals	Positive and Negative affect	Four modalities – 80 Two modalities - 79
Chao *et al*. [46]	2021	CNN	Univariate Convolution layer Multivariate Convolution layer Fully connected layer	EEG	Valence (2), Arousal (2) HAHV, LAHV, LALV, HALV (4)	Binary class- 85.53 (V), 85.88 (A) Four class- 76.77
Gao *et al*. [47]	2020	CNN	1 Convolution layer 3 Dense blocks 2 Transition blocks	EEG	Valence (2), Arousal (2)	SEED – 90.63 DEAP – 92.24 (V), 92.92 (A)
Zhong *et al*. [48]	2020	CNN	CNN - input layers, hidden layers, and output layers 2 hidden Markov models	EEG	Arousal (2), Valence (2), Dominance (2)	79.77 (A), 83.09 (V) and 81.83 (D)
Hwang *et al*. [49]	2020	CNN	2 Convolution layers 2 Max Pooling layers 4 Linear layers	EEG	Positive, Negative and Neutral	90.41
Sarkar *et al* [50]	2020	Multi-task CNN	3 Convolutional blocks Task-specific layer with 2 dense and 7 parallel tasks	ECG	Valence (2), Arousal (2)	AMIGOS - 88.9 (A), 87.5 (V) DREAMER – 85.9 (A), 85.0 (V)

CONCLUSION

This chapter provides in-depth knowledge about multimodal emotion representation. It also deals with various modalities used for emotion representation. It provides detailed descriptions of prime modalities like audio, video, and physiological signals. The fundamentals of facial emotion recognition are also discussed in detail, along with noticeable studies of facial emotion recognition using different algorithms.

REFERENCES

[1] K. Schaaff, EEG-based emotion recognition., Ph.D. thesis, Universitat Karlsruhe (TH), 2008.

[2] P. Ekman, W.V. Friesen, M. O'Sullivan, A. Chan, I. Diacoyanni-Tarlatzis, K. Heider, R. Krause, W.A. LeCompte, T. Pitcairn, P.E. Ricci-Bitti, K. Scherer, M. Tomita, and A. Tzavaras, "Universals and cultural differences in the judgments of facial expressions of emotion", *J. Pers. Soc. Psychol.,* vol. 53, no. 4, pp. 712-717, 1987. [http://dx.doi.org/10.1037/0022-3514.53.4.712] [PMID: 3681648]

[3] S. Koelstra, A. Yazdani, M. Soleymani, and C. Mü, "Single trial classification of EEG and peripheral physiological signals for recognition of emotions induced by music videos", In: *Proc. Brain Informatics*, 2010, pp. 89-100.

[4] A. Jaimes, and N. Sebe, "Multimodal human-computer interaction: A survey", *Computer Vision and Image Understanding,* vol. 108, no. 1, pp. 116-134, 2007. [http://dx.doi.org/10.1016/j.cviu.2006.10.019]

[5] G.K. Verma, and B.K. Singh, "Facial emotion recognition in curvelet domain", *Commun. Comput. Inf. Sci.,* vol. 157, pp. 554-559, 2011. [http://dx.doi.org/10.1007/978-3-642-22786-8_70]

[6] N. Sebe, I. Cohen, A. Garg, and T.S. Huang, *Machine Learning in Computer Vision.* Springer: Berlin, NY, 2005.

[7] B. Fehr, and J.A. Russell, "Concept of emotion viewed from a prototype perspective", *J. Exp. Psychol. Gen.,* vol. 113, no. 3, pp. 464-486, 1984. [http://dx.doi.org/10.1037/0096-3445.113.3.464]

[8] P.R. Kleinginna Jr, and A.M. Kleinginna, "A categorized list of emotion definitions, with suggestions for a consensual definition", *Motiv. Emot.,* vol. 5, no. 4, pp. 345-379, 1981. [http://dx.doi.org/10.1007/BF00992553]

[9] S. Moharreri, N.J. Dabanloo, S. Parvaneh, and A.M. Nasrabadi, "The relation between colors, emotions and heart using Triangle Phase Space Mapping (TPSM)", *Comput. Cardiol.,* p. 38, 2011.

[10] N. Hadjikhani, and B. de Gelder, "Seeing fearful body expressions activates the fusiform cortex and amygdala", *Curr. Biol.,* vol. 13, no. 24, pp. 2201-2205, 2003. [http://dx.doi.org/10.1016/j.cub.2003.11.049] [PMID: 14680638]

[11] P. Ekaterina, Volkova, Betty J. Mohler, Trevor J. Dodds, Joachim Tesch, P. Ekaterina, and Heinrich H. Bülthoff, "Emotion categorization of body expressions in narrative scenarios", *Front. Psychol.,* 2014.

[12] Charles Darwin, *The Expression of the Emotions in Man and Animals*, 1872. [http://dx.doi.org/10.1037/10001-000]

[13] "Language and the politics of emotion", In: *Studies in Emotion and Social Interaction*Cambridge University Press, New York, 1990.

[14] P. Ekman, "Facial expression and emotion", *Am Psychol,* vol. 48, no. 4, pp. 384-92, 1993. [http://dx.doi.org/10.1037/0003-066X.48.4.384]

[15] R.M. Nesse, "Evolutionary explanations of emotions", *Hum. Nat.,* vol. 1, no. 3, pp. 261-289, 1990. [http://dx.doi.org/10.1007/BF02733986] [PMID: 24222085]

[16] P. Ekman, and W. Friesen, *Facial Action Coding System: A Technique for the Measurement of Facial Movement.* Consulting Psychologists Press: Palo Alto, 1978.

[17] H. Bindu Maringanti, P. Gupta, and U.S. Tiwari, "Cognitive model-based emotion recognition from facial expressions for live computer interaction", In: *IEEE symposium on Computational Intelligence in Image and Signal Processing (CIISP)*, 2007.

[18] J.M. Fellous, "From human emotions to robot emotions", *American Association for Artificial*

Intelligence, Spring Symposium, 2004

[19] Y. Jingfu, Y. Zhan, and S. Song, "Facial expression features extraction based on Gabor wavelet transformation", *International Conference on Systems, Man and Cybernetics,* vol. 3, 2004pp. 2215-2219 [http://dx.doi.org/10.1109/ICSMC.2004.1400657]

[20] N. Matthew, Dailey, and Garrison W. Cottrell, "EMPATH: A neural network that categorizes facial expressions", *J. Cogn. Neurosci.,* vol. 14, no. 8, pp. 1158-1173, 2002.

[21] L.A. Axelrod, Emotional recognition in computing, Ph.D. Thesis, Brunel University, School of Information Systems, Computing and Mathematics, 2011.

[22] T. Sha, M. Song, J. Bu, C. Chen, and D. Tao, "Feature level analysis for 3D facial expression recognition", *Neurocomputing,* vol. 74, no. 12-13, pp. 2135-2141, 2011. [http://dx.doi.org/10.1016/j.neucom.2011.01.008]

[23] H. Soyel, and H. Demirel, "Optimal feature selection for 3D facial expression recognition using coarse-to-fine classification", *Turk. J. Electr. Eng. Comput. Sci.,* vol. 18, no. 6, pp. 1031-1040, 2010. [http://dx.doi.org/10.3906/elk-0908-158]

[24] H. Soyel, and H. Demirel, "Optimal feature selection for 3D facial expression recognition with geometrically localized facial features", *Fifth International Conference on Soft Computing, Computing with Words and Perceptions in System Analysis, Decision and Control, ICSCCW 2009,* 2009pp. 1-4 [http://dx.doi.org/10.1109/ICSCCW.2009.5379476]

[25] R. Srivastava, and S. Roy, "3D facial expression recognition using residues", In: *TENCON-2009, IEEE Region 10 Conference*, 2009, pp. 1-5.

[26] A. Savran, B. Sankur, and M. Taha Bilge, "Comparative evaluation of 3D vs. 2D modality for automatic detection of facial action units", *Pattern Recognit.,* vol. 45, no. 2, pp. 767-782, 2012. [http://dx.doi.org/10.1016/j.patcog.2011.07.022]

[27] Loong-Fah Cheong, L.F. Cheong, and Hee Lin Wang, "Affective understanding in film", *IEEE Trans. Circ. Syst. Video Tech.,* vol. 16, no. 6, pp. 689-704, 2006. [http://dx.doi.org/10.1109/TCSVT.2006.873781]

[28] P. Lemaire, "Fully automatic 3Dfacial expression recognition using a region-based approach", *Proceedings of the 2011 Joint ACM Workshop on Human Gesture and Behavior Understanding, J-HGBU'11, ACM New York,* 2011pp. 53-58

[29] A. Maalej, B.B. Amor, M. Daoudi, A. Srivastava, and S. Berretti, "Shape analysis of local facial patches for 3D facial expression recognition", *Pattern Recognit.,* vol. 44, no. 8, pp. 1581-1589, 2011. [http://dx.doi.org/10.1016/j.patcog.2011.02.012]

[30] S. Berretti, B. Ben Amor, M. Daoudi, and A. del Bimbo, "3D facial expression recognition using SIFT descriptors of automatically detected keypoints", *Vis. Comput.,* vol. 27, no. 11, pp. 1021-1036, 2011. [http://dx.doi.org/10.1007/s00371-011-0611-x]

[31] Y. Wu, M. Xia, L. Nie, Y. Zhang, and A. Fan, "Simultaneously exploring multi-scale and asymmetric EEG features for emotion recognition", *Comput. Biol. Med.,* vol. 149, 2022.106002 [http://dx.doi.org/10.1016/j.compbiomed.2022.106002] [PMID: 36041272]

[32] Yuqi Wang, "EEG-based emotion recognition using a 2D CNN with different kernels", *Bioengineering 9.6,* vol. 231, 2022. [http://dx.doi.org/10.3390/bioengineering9060231]

[33] G. Bao, K. Yang, L. Tong, J. Shu, R. Zhang, L. Wang, B. Yan, and Y. Zeng, "Linking multi-layer dynamical GCN with style-based recalibration CNN for EEG-based emotion recognition", *Front. Neurorobot.,* vol. 16, 2022.834952 [http://dx.doi.org/10.3389/fnbot.2022.834952] [PMID: 35280845]

[34] He Wang, "A gradient-based automatic optimization CNN framework for EEG state recognition", *J.*

Neural Eng., vol. 19.1, p. 016009, 2022.
[http://dx.doi.org/10.1088/1741-2552/ac41ac]

[35] J. Hu, C. Wang, Q. Jia, Q. Bu, R. Sutcliffe, and J. Feng, "ScalingNet: Extracting features from raw EEG data for emotion recognition", *Neurocomputing,* vol. 463, pp. 177-184, 2021.
[http://dx.doi.org/10.1016/j.neucom.2021.08.018]

[36] X. Zheng, X. Yu, Y. Yin, T. Li, and X. Yan, "Three-dimensional feature maps and convolutional neural network-based emotion recognition", *Int. J. Intell. Syst.,* vol. 36, no. 11, pp. 6312-6336, 2021.
[http://dx.doi.org/10.1002/int.22551]

[37] M.R. Islam, M.M. Islam, M.M. Rahman, C. Mondal, S.K. Singha, M. Ahmad, A. Awal, M.S. Islam, and M.A. Moni, "EEG channel correlation based model for emotion recognition", *Comput. Biol. Med.,* vol. 136, 2021.104757
[http://dx.doi.org/10.1016/j.compbiomed.2021.104757] [PMID: 34416570]

[38] E.S. Salama, R.A. El-Khoribi, M.E. Shoman, and M.A. Wahby Shalaby, "A 3D-convolutional neural network framework with ensemble learning techniques for multi-modal emotion recognition", *Egyptian Informatics Journal,* vol. 22, no. 2, pp. 167-176, 2021.
[http://dx.doi.org/10.1016/j.eij.2020.07.005]

[39] N. Ganapathy, Y.R. Veeranki, H. Kumar, and R. Swaminathan, "Emotion recognition using electrodermal activity signals and multiscale deep convolutional neural network", *J. Med. Syst.,* vol. 45, no. 4, p. 49, 2021.
[http://dx.doi.org/10.1007/s10916-020-01676-6] [PMID: 33660087]

[40] Mehmet Akif Ozdemir, "EEG-based emotion recognition with deep convolutional neural networks", *Biomed Tech,* pp. 43-57, 2021.
[http://dx.doi.org/10.1515/bmt-2019-0306]

[41] L. Zhou, "Analysis of psychological and emotional tendency based on brain functional imaging and deep learning", *Discrete Dyn. Nat. Soc.,* vol. 2021, pp. 1-9, 2021.
[http://dx.doi.org/10.1155/2021/1272502]

[42] S. Garg, "An overlapping sliding window and combined features based emotion recognition system for EEG signals", In: *Applied Computing and Informatics*, 2021.
[http://dx.doi.org/10.1108/ACI-05-2021-0130]

[43] S. Liu, X. Wang, L. Zhao, B. Li, W. Hu, J. Yu, and Y. Zhang, "3DCANN: a spatio-temporal convolution attention neural network for EEG emotion recognition", *IEEE J. Biomed. Health Inform.,* vol. PP, p. 1, 2021.
[http://dx.doi.org/10.1109/JBHI.2021.3083525] [PMID: 34033551]

[44] Y. Chen, R. Chang, and J. Guo, "Effects of data augmentation method borderline-SMOTE on emotion recognition of EEG signals based on convolutional neural network", *IEEE Access,* vol. 9, pp. 47491-47502, 2021.
[http://dx.doi.org/10.1109/ACCESS.2021.3068316]

[45] M.D. Hssayeni, and B. Ghoraani, "Multi-modal physiological data fusion for affect estimation using deep learning", *IEEE Access,* vol. 9, pp. 21642-21652, 2021.
[http://dx.doi.org/10.1109/ACCESS.2021.3055933]

[46] H. Chao, and L. Dong, "Emotion recognition using three-dimensional feature and convolutional neural network from multichannel EEG signals", *IEEE Sens. J.,* vol. 21, no. 2, pp. 2024-2034, 2021.
[http://dx.doi.org/10.1109/JSEN.2020.3020828]

[47] Z. Gao, "A channel-fused dense convolutional network for EEG-based emotion recognition", *IEEE Trans. Cogn. Dev. Syst.,* 2020.

[48] Q. Zhong, Y. Zhu, D. Cai, L. Xiao, and H. Zhang, "Electroencephalogram access for emotion recognition based on a deep hybrid network", *Front. Hum. Neurosci.,* vol. 14, 2020.589001
[http://dx.doi.org/10.3389/fnhum.2020.589001] [PMID: 33390918]

[49] S. Hwang, K. Hong, G. Son, and H. Byun, "Learning CNN features from DE features for EEG-based emotion recognition", *Pattern Anal. Appl.,* vol. 23, no. 3, pp. 1323-1335, 2020. [http://dx.doi.org/10.1007/s10044-019-00860-w]

[50] P. Sarkar, and A. Etemad, "Self-supervised ECG representation learning for emotion recognition", *IEEE Trans. Affect. Comput.,* 2020.

CHAPTER 3

Models and Theory of Emotion

Abstract: This chapter presents a state-of-the-art review of existing emotion theory, modeling approaches, and affective information extraction and processing methods. The basic theory of emotions deals with Darwin's evolutionary theory, Schechter's theory of emotion, and James–Lange's theory. These theories are fundamental building blocks of Affective Computing research. Emotion modeling approaches can be categorized into categorical, appraisal, and dimensional models. Noticeable contributions to Affect recognition systems in terms of modality, database, and dimensionality are also discussed in this chapter.

Keywords: Appraisal model, Categorical model, Dimensional model, Emotion modeling, Emotion theory.

3.1. INTRODUCTION

Modeling emotion is essential for a better understanding of emotions. Efficient modeling of emotions is still challenging due to the involvement of various emotional modalities. As each modality has a different pattern, emotion modeling depends upon the type of input signals. Emotion theories and models are the basis for gaining in-depth knowledge about the induction of emotions. Researchers have proposed many emotion theories; among them, the James-Lange theory, Canon-Bard theory, and Schachter-Singer theory of emotion contributed significantly.

The emotional state of a human being at a particular moment is the combination of the user's physiological, psychological, and subjective experience [1]. The appraisal experience depends on various parameters, such as growing environment, background, and culture. Thus, people feel different experiences of similar phenomena or events.

3.2. EMOTION THEORY

The three primary emotion models are the category, appraisal-based, and dimensional models [2].

Gyanendra K. Verma

The category model is concerned with universally recognized basic emotions. The number of these basic emotions is modest, yet they are all linked to our brains [3]. The appraisal-based approach deals with modelling emotions as a physiological response to stimuli or events that leads to the emergence of emotion and associated action. On a continuous or discrete scale, dimensional methods describe emotion through some independent dimensions. Fig. (**3.1**) depicts various emotion theories.

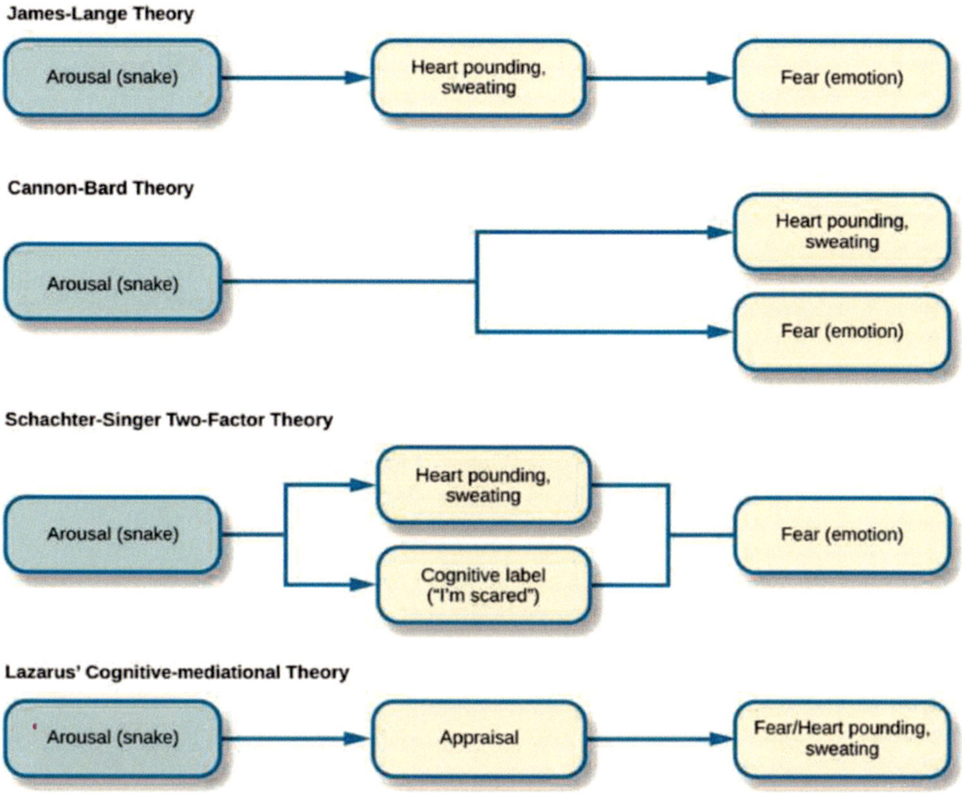

Fig.(3.1). Major emotion theories.

3.2.1. Categorical Approach

Prof. P. Ekman made significant contributions in the area of Emotion Recognition. He was the first to introduce six basic emotions visible in facial expressions [4]. Fig. (**3.2**) illustrates the six primary emotions proposed by Ekman. In 1980, Robert Plutchik introduced the "Wheel of emotion," a new notion of emotion [5]. Fig. (**3.2**) classified a few feelings as core emotions: joy, sorrow, anger, fear, trust, contempt, surprise, and anticipation. In 2001, Parrot offered a classification of emotion, which Robert Plutchik followed.

Fig. (3.2). Ekman's six universal emotions.

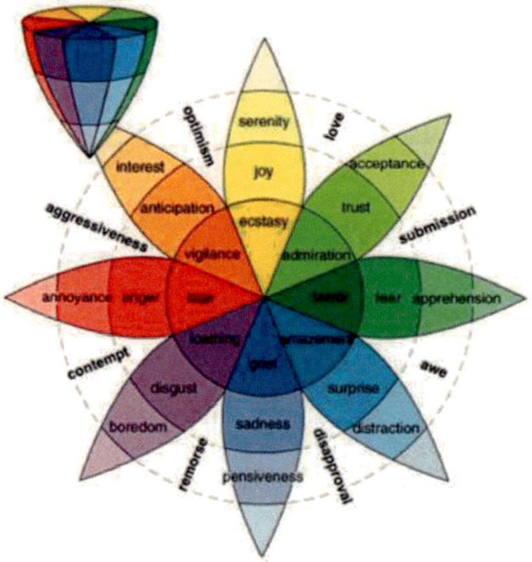

Fig. (3.3). Robert Plutchik's Wheel of emotion [8].

The idea of Parrot was to divide emotions into three categories: primary, secondary, and tertiary [6]. There are six significant emotions, twenty-five secondary emotions, and more than tertiary ones in Parrots' hypothesis. Among the different theories of emotions published in the literature, Plutchik and Conte's [7] study is the most noteworthy. The "Psycho-evolutionary Theory of Emotions" was created by them. Robert Plutchik's wheel of emotion [8] is shown in Figure **(3.3)**

3.2.2. Evolutionary Theory of Emotion by Darwin

Ekman [9] defined the six primary emotions as "happy," "sad," "angry," "fear," "surprise," and "disgust." These six fundamental emotions are based on Darwin's evolutionary perspective [10]. According to Darwin's theory, some essential components of emotions are biologically grounded and genetically determined. The fundamental emotions originated first in species. Subsequently, more emotions were generated by refining these emotions as evolution progressed.

Fig. (**3.4**) shows Russell's circumplex model of affect, which is based on emotional states of brain experiences that result from two separate neurophysiological systems. He plotted structures in two dimensions at first: A circular depiction of activation (the degree of strength or arousal of emotion) and Pleasantness (the valence - how positive or negative the feeling is).

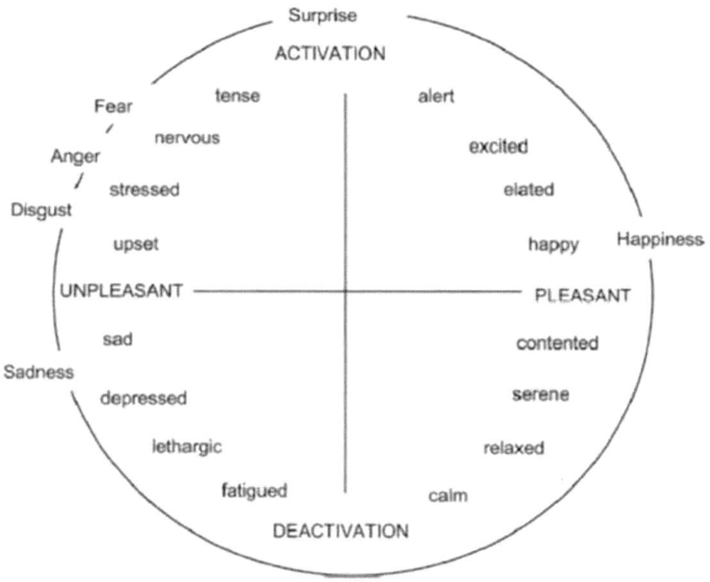

Fig. (3.4). Russell's circumplex model of affect.

3.2.3. Cognitive Appraisal and Physiological Theory of Emotions

According to Schachter's theory of emotion [11], the physiological changes induced by the human body when it recognizes stimuli and causally connects stimulation to the cognized source. Schachter's theory supports the other theories of cognitive evaluation as proposed by Lazarus *et al.* in 1980. Cognitive evaluations are characterized by fleeting pleasure, certainty, situational control, and attentional engagement. The cognitive evaluation of events contributing to emotional experience is established by [12]. According to the James- Lange theory, emotion is a response to physiological changes in our bodies caused by stimuli [13]. The physiological processes in our bodies prior to arousal vary for different emotions. Analyzing emotion will be much easier if we understand the physiological changes in our bodies. Sundberg *et al.* [14] described how they used a physiology-driven method to analyze emotion. They have presented a concept of action units that work together to create a particular facial expression.

A huge question in emotion theory was defined by [15]. Whether physiological patterns are adequate to follow each emotion as physiological muscle movements, they believe, is an unresolved topic. To the untrained eye, what seems to be a facial expression may not necessarily reflect an actual emotional state?

3.2.4. Dimensional Approaches to Emotions

Emotion categorization is a high-level module for understanding human affective states in emotion recognition. The continuous-valued scale is one method for classification since it may represent the intensity of emotions [16]. Humans not only sense emotions but also their intensity, such as being highly sad or less pleased.

The dimensional method represents a given level of emotional intensity in n-dimensional space, usually 2D or 3D. The most popular 3D space is Valence, Arousal, and Dominance (VAD). Few researchers used Pleasure, Arousal, and Dominance in the literature [17] (PAD). The valence scale spans from disagreeable to agreeable. Kolestra *et al.* [18] incorporated more emotional space, such as like, into their study [16]. Table **3.1** contains a list of related works.

Wang and Cheong *et al.* [19] introduced a multimodal emotion recognition system based on a probabilistic inference approach. The characteristics are based on psychological and cinematographic principles. They classified 36 full-length movies into 2040 scenes with the help of a support vector machine.

S. Arifin *et al.* [17] suggested a method for extracting emotion from movies automatically. They employed an affective video content analysis model based on the Hierarchical Dynamic Bayesian Network (HDBN) to extract affective level information.

The emotional scene of the film was then determined using a spectral clustering method. For affect representation, they used the pleasure-arousal-dominance (PAD) dimensions. The system's performance was compared to the time adaptive clustering technique. They employed six emotion categories, one for each video, and 10790 video segments retrieved from 43 videos.

Table 3.1. Affect recognition systems by modality, database, and dimensionality.

Study	Mode	Database	Number of Samples	Dimensions
M. Nicolaou at el [3].	Audiovisual	SAL database	2 male and 2 female subjects	Arousal-valence
B. Schuller *et al.* [16]	Audio	Multi-databases	Various no. for different databases	Arousal-valence
Arifin *et al.* [17]	audiovisual	Self-collected	10970 shots and 762 video segments	Ekman's emotion
Wang *et al.* [19]	Audio-visual	Self-collected	2040 scenes from 36 movie	Seven emotion categories
Zhang *et al.* [20]	Audio-visual	Self-collected	552 music videos	Arousal & valence score
Soleymani *et al.*1 [21]	Audio-visual	Self-collected	64 movie scenes from 8 movies	Arousal and valence self-assessment
Soleymani *et al.*2 [22]	Audio-visual	Self-collected	21 movies	Arousal & valence
Canini *et al.* [25]	audiovisual	Self-collected	240 subjects, 25 movie scenes	Three connotative dimensions
Irie *et al.* [26]	audiovisual	Self-collected	206 scenes (24 movies titles)	Ekman's emotion

Zhang *et al.* [20] suggested a method for achieving individualized emotional analysis by combining support vector regression with an affective psychological model. They developed a customized emotional model using an MTV video based on arousal computation using a linear combination of arousal and valence parameters.

Soleymani M. *et al.* [21] found links between multimedia characteristics, physiological features, and valence-arousal self-assessment. They employed a dataset of 64 movie sequences from eight Hollywood films. Later, they introduced an audio-visual features-based Bayesian framework for video emotional representation [22].

Using Hidden Markov Models, N. Malandrakis *et al.* [23] proposed a supervised learning method to model the continuous affective response (HMM). The model is meant to categorize video frames into seven discrete categories. Then spline interpolation is used to transform discrete values into continuous values.

They experimented with 30-minute movie snippets by combining unproven theory with clustering, L. Yan *et al.* [24] suggested a content-based method for recognizing emotional video content. A video scenario assessed brightness, shot cut-rate, and color effectiveness as low-level attributes. They created an unconfirmed video clustering model, then used a way to set the index weight of each emotion characteristic and clustered the video. They used 112 video sequences from four different films.

L. Canini *et al.* [25] suggested an emotional framework for describing movies' connotative features in terms of affect. Connotation, according to Canini, is an intermediate representation that uses the objectivity of audio-visual descriptions to anticipate users' subjective emotional reactions. They create a link between audio-visual characteristics and connotative rates.

According to Mihalis [3], emotions are systematically connected in the dimensional approach. A given affective state is a mix of each dimension. The three aspects of valence, arousal, and dominance have been studied extensively. The valence dimension (V), which spans from dissatisfied to cheerful, quantifies emotion in terms of positive or negative emotion. The arousal component (A) runs from bored to enthusiastic, whereas dominance assesses submissiveness (control) to empowerment (controlled). Arousal and valence have been linked in studies by [26, 27, 28]. Fontaine [29] proposed four dimensions to define diverse emotions: valence, potency, arousal and unpredictability.

Affective states, according to Whissell [30], Russell [31], and Plutchik [5], are not independent but are systematically associated. They propose a continuous two-dimensional space with two dimensions for evaluation and activation. The appraisal dimension evaluates human emotion and goes from good to negative. The activation dimension assesses whether people are more or less prone to act in response to their emotions. Fig. (**3.5**) depicts a two-dimensional evaluation-activation space that ranges from active to inactive.

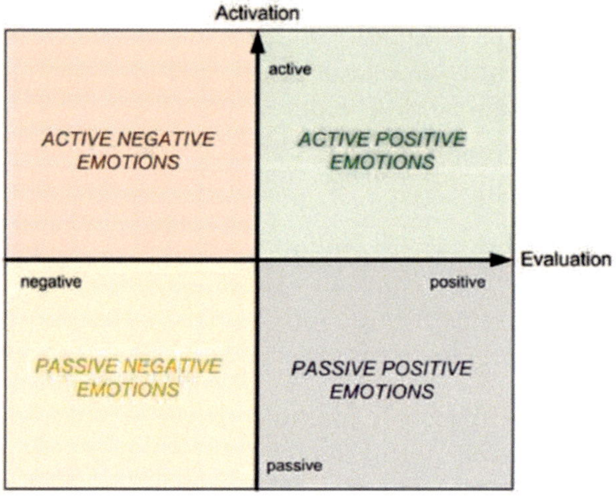

Fig. (3.5). 2D evaluation-activation spaces.

CONCLUSION

This chapter presented the different theories of emotion, starting from Darwin's theory of evolution to Lazarus' cognitive-mediational theory. The three most categories of emotion, *i.e.*, appraisal, psychological and cognitive aspects of emotion discussed. Modeling of emotion, including Russell's circumplex model of emotion and Plutchiks' wheel of emotion has also been discussed. The noticeable research on emotion theory and models is also reviewed systematically.

REFERENCES

[1] C.J. Beedie, P.C. Terry, A.M. Lane, and T.J. Devonport, "Differential assessment of emotions and moods: development and validation of the emotion and mood components of anxiety questionnaire", *Pers. Individ. Dif.*, vol. 50, no. 2, pp. 228-233, 2011. [http://dx.doi.org/10.1016/j.paid.2010.09.034]

[2] D. Grandjean, D. Sander, and K.R. Scherer, "Conscious emotional experience emerges as a function of multilevel, appraisal-driven response synchronization", *Conscious. Cogn.*, vol. 17, no. 2, pp. 484-495, 2008. [http://dx.doi.org/10.1016/j.concog.2008.03.019] [PMID: 18448361]

[3] M.A. Nicolaou, H. Gunes, and M. Pantic, "Continuous prediction of spontaneous affect from multiple cues and modalities in valence-arousal space", *IEEE Trans. Affect. Comput.*, vol. 2, no. 2, pp. 92-105, 2011. [http://dx.doi.org/10.1109/T-AFFC.2011.9]

[4] P. Ekman, "Facial expression and emotion", *American Psychologist,* vol. 384, no. 392, 1993. [http://dx.doi.org/10.1037/0003-066X.48.4.384]

[5] R. Plutchik, *Emotion: a Psycho-evolutionary Synthesis.* Harper & Row, 1980.

[6] W. Parrott, *Emotions in Social Psychology.* Psychology Press: Philadelphia, 2001.

[7] R. Plutchik, and R. Conte, *Hope, "Circumplex Models of Personality and Emotions".* American Psychological Association: Washington, 1997. [http://dx.doi.org/10.1037/10261-000]

[8] R. Plutchik, "A psycho-evolutionary theory of emotions", *Soc. Sci. Inf. (Paris),* vol. 21, no. 4–5, pp. 529-553, 2008.

[9] P. Ekman, "Basic emotions", In: *Handbook of Cognition and Emotion*, 1999, pp. 45-60. [http://dx.doi.org/10.1002/0470013494.ch3]

[10] Charles Darwin, *The expression of the emotions in man and animals,* 18721988. [http://dx.doi.org/10.1037/10001-000]

[11] S. Schachter, and J. Singer, "Cognitive, social, and physiological determinants of emotional state", *Psychol. Rev.*, vol. 69, no. 5, pp. 379-399, 1962. [http://dx.doi.org/10.1037/h0046234] [PMID: 14497895]

[12] C.A. Smith, and P.C. Ellsworth, "Patterns of cognitive appraisal in emotion", *J. Pers. Soc. Psychol.*, vol. 48, no. 4, pp. 813-838, 1985. [http://dx.doi.org/10.1037/0022-3514.48.4.813] [PMID: 3886875]

[13] W. James, *The Principles of Psychology.* vol. Vol. 1. Dover Publications, 1950.

[14] J. Sundberg, S. Patel, E. Bjorkner, and K.R. Scherer, "Interdependencies among Voice Source Parameters in Emotional Speech", *IEEE Trans. Affect. Comput.*, vol. 2, no. 3, pp. 162-174, 2011.

[http://dx.doi.org/10.1109/T-AFFC.2011.14]

[15] J.T. Cacioppo, and L.G. Tassinary, "Inferring psychological significance from physiological signals", *Am. Psychol.,* vol. 45, no. 1, pp. 16-28, 1990. [http://dx.doi.org/10.1037/0003-066X.45.1.16] [PMID: 2297166]

[16] B. Schuller, "Recognizing affect from linguistic information in 3d continuous space", *IEEE Trans. Affect. Comput.,* vol. 2, no. 4, pp. 192-205, 2011. [http://dx.doi.org/10.1109/T-AFFC.2011.17]

[17] S. Arifin, and P.Y.K. Cheung, "Affective level video segmentation by utilizing the pleasure-arousa--dominance information", *IEEE Trans. Multimed.,* vol. 10, no. 7, pp. 1325-1341, 2008. [http://dx.doi.org/10.1109/TMM.2008.2004911]

[18] S. Koelstra, C. Muhl, M. Soleymani, Jong-Seok Lee, A. Yazdani, T. Ebrahimi, T. Pun, A. Nijholt, and I. Patras, "DEAP: A database for emotion analysis; using physiological signals", *IEEE Trans. Affect. Comput.,* vol. 3, no. 1, pp. 18-31, 2012. [http://dx.doi.org/10.1109/T-AFFC.2011.15]

[19] Loong-Fah Cheong, L.F. Cheong, and H.L. Wang, "Affective understanding in film", *IEEE Trans. Circ. Syst. Video Tech.,* vol. 16, no. 6, pp. 689-704, 2006. [http://dx.doi.org/10.1109/TCSVT.2006.873781]

[20] S. Zhang, Q. Huang, Q. Tian, S. Jiang, and W. Gao, "“Personalized MTV affective analysis using user profile", In: *Advances in Multimedia Information Processing.* vol. 5353. Springer: Berlin Heidelberg, 2008, pp. 327-337.

[21] M. Soleymani, "A multimodal database for affect recognition and implicit tagging", In: *IEEE Tran. On Affective Computing* vol. 3. , 2012no. 1, . 2012a

[22] M. Soleymani, M. Pantic, T. Pun, and M. Pantic, "Multimodal Emotion Recognition in Response to Videos", *IEEE Trans. Affect. Comput.,* vol. 3, no. 2, pp. 211-223, 2012. b [http://dx.doi.org/10.1109/T-AFFC.2011.37]

[23] N. Malandrakis, A. Potamianos, G. Evangelopoulos, and A. Zlatintsi, "A supervised approach to movie emotion tracking", , pp. 2376-379, 2011. [http://dx.doi.org/10.1109/ICASSP.2011.5946961]

[24] L. Yan, X. Wen, and W. Zheng, "Study on unascertained clustering for video affective recognition", *JICS,* vol. 8, no. 13, pp. 2865-2873, 2011.

[25] L. Canini, S. Benini, and R. Leonardi, "Affective recommendation of movies based on selected connotative features", *Circuits and Systems for Video Technology, IEEE Transactions,* vol. 23, no. 4, pp. 636-647, 2013. [http://dx.doi.org/10.1109/TCSVT.2012.2211935]

[26] G. Irie, T. Satou, A. Kojima, T. Yamasaki, and K. Aizawa, "Affective audio-visual words and latent topic driving model for realizing movie affective scene classification", *IEEE Trans. Multimed.,* vol. 12, no. 6, pp. 523-535, 2010. [http://dx.doi.org/10.1109/TMM.2010.2051871]

[27] A.M. Oliveira, M.P. Teixeira, I.B. Fonseca, and M. Oliveira, "Joint model-parameter validation of valence and arousal: Probing a differential weighting model of affective intensity", *Proceedings of Fechner Day,* vol. 22, pp. 245-250, 2006.

[28] P. Lewis, H. Critchley, P. Rotshtein, and R. Dolan, "Neural correlates of processing valence and arousal in affective words", *Cereb. Cortex,* vol. 17, no. 3, pp. 742-748, 2006. [http://dx.doi.org/10.1093/cercor/bhk024] [PMID: 16699082]

[29] J.R.J. Fontaine, K.R. Scherer, E.B. Roesch, and P.C. Ellsworth, "The world of emotions is not two-dimensional", *Psychol. Sci.,* vol. 18, no. 12, pp. 1050-1057, 2007. [http://dx.doi.org/10.1111/j.1467-9280.2007.02024.x] [PMID: 18031411]

[30] C.M. Whissell, *The dictionary of affect in language, emotion: Theory, research and experience.* vol. Vol. 4. Academic Press: New York, 1989.

[31] J.A. Russell, "A circumplex model of affect", *J. Pers. Soc. Psychol.,* vol. 39, no. 6, pp. 1161-1178, 1980.
[http://dx.doi.org/10.1037/h0077714]

CHAPTER 4

Affective Information Extraction, Processing and Evaluation

Abstract: This chapter presents a state-of-the-art review of existing affective information extraction and processing approaches. Various evaluation criteria, such as Evaluation matrices like ROC, F1 measure, Mean Square Error, Mean Average Error, Threshold criteria, and Performance criteria are also reported in this chapter.

Keywords: Evaluation measures, F1 measures, Information extraction, ROC curve.

4.1. INTRODUCTION

Information extraction from multimodal cues is usually used as complementary. When getting the information from one cue is terminated, the system may shift to other traits and continue its functioning. There are three primary sources of affective information: speech, images or videos, and text. The first two cues, *i.e.*, speech and images, are widely used for affective information processing. However, text-based affective information analysis targets specific applications and comes under Natural Language Processing (NLP) domain [1]. Where information processing is concerned, the time-series data is easy to process and extract. Usually, the audio and image information is synchronized in a time-dependent manner.

4.2. AFFECTIVE INFORMATION EXTRACTION AND PROCESSING

4.2.1. Information Extraction from Audio

Diverse speech aspects, such as mood, speaker audio, and both, are used to represent different speech information. As a result, experts are interested in learning more about the speech characteristics of various emotions. Vocal tract, prosodic, and excitation source characteristics are the three types of speech features. Short segments of voice signals are used to extract Vocal Tract characteristics. The energy distribution for a variety of speech frequencies is

Gyanendra K. Verma

represented by these properties. Various vocal tract elements and their combinations are employed by various studies for emotion identification. T. Long [2] employed a mixture of Perceptual Linear Prediction (PLP), MFCC, and LPCC to distinguish emotions, such as angry, happy, sad, bored, and neutral, using the log frequency power coefficient (LFPC) vocal tract feature. As pitch has a higher discriminating power than other prosodic variables, it is the most extensively employed prosodic feature for emotion identification. Aside from pitch, log energy is a popular metric for analysing speaking styles and emotions.

4.2.2. Information Extraction from Video

The appearance of changes owing to lighting and position fluctuations complicates geometric feature-based face analysis. Hence, spatio-temporal characteristics can be utilised to identify minor changes in a face. The interest spots in picture sequences are detected using Dollar's approach [3]. This approach was created to identify minor changes in the spatial and temporal domains in which the human action recognition community is most interested. Multiresolution techniques may also be used to extract visual information from photographs.

4.2.3. Information Extraction from Physiological Signals

Physiological signals are vital for emotion, according to several emotion theories. Ekman established that a certain emotion may be linked to a specific physiological pattern. The frequency and amplitude of an EEG signal can be used to characterize it.

To split the physiological signal into distinct frequency bands, a bandpass filter can be utilised. Discrete Wavelet Transform is another approach for decomposing EEG signals into distinct frequency bands (DWT). Galvanic Skin Response (GSR), respiration amplitude, electrocardiogram (ECG), electromyograms (EMG), electrooculogram (EOG), Electro dermal Activity (EDA), Galvanic Skin Response (GSR), Skin Conductance Response (SCR), and skin temperature are examples of peripheral biosignals. EDA and GSR are skin conductance measurements that are extensively utilised for automated emotion identification. GSR is a fairly reliable physiological marker of human arousal, according to J. Kim [4].

4.3. STUDIES ON AFFECT INFORMATION PROCESSING

People use various modes of communication in day-to-day interaction with others. We can broadly categorize these communication modes into verbal and non-verbal communication. Verbal communication involves speech and audio; however, non-verbal communication uses facial expressions, body gestures, and sign language. Both communication modes are vital and play a significant role in communication among human beings. Unfortunately, we lack a better human-computer interface to use these vital communication channels. Facial expressions are essential to recognize sentiments in communications. Koelstra *et al.* [5] discovered substantial changes in N400 ERP responses when placing relevant and irrelevant tags on short videos. They started by extracting features from audio and video channels. Then, the correlation between audio and visual properties was investigated using the method described above. After that, a hidden Markov model is utilized to characterize statistical dependency across time segments and discover the features in the altered domain's fundamental temporal structure. Extensive system testing is used to assess the resilience of our suggested solution.

Emotion identification can be unimodal or multimodal. The unimodal-based method uses a single modality to recognize the emotion. In contrast, the multimodel technique collects emotional information from several inputs, such as audio, video, image, physiological signals, *etc*. We have dealt with multimodel emotion recognition in this study. Several researchers also used this multimodel strategy. S. Koelstra *et al.* [5] suggested a facial expression and EEG signal fusion system for emotion identification using multimodal fusion.

Mamalis A. Nikolaou [6] demonstrated a multimodal emotion identification system that combines facial expressions, shoulder gestures, and aural signals. They used two-dimensional spaces of valence and arousal to map multimodal emotions on a continuous scale. Further, an associative fusion framework was presented using Support Vector Regression (SVR) and Long Short Term Memory neural networks (BLSTM-NNs).

Y. Wang *et al.* [7] used the kernel approach to examine multimodal information extraction and analysis. For modeling the nonlinear interaction between two multidimensional variables, they used Kernel cross-modal factor analysis. They have also developed a method for determining the best transformations to describe patterns.

M. Paleri *et al.* [8] published a paper on feature selection for automated audio-visual person-independent emotion identification. They employed a neural network to compare the performance of different characteristics in an emotion identification system.

M. Mansoorizadeh [9] suggested an asynchronous feature-level fusion strategy for the assimilation of speech and facial expressions using a unified hybrid feature space. They stated that the suggested fusion strategy outperforms a system based only on face and voice. The outcome was compared with existing studies regarding feature and decision-level fusion.

Datchu *et al.* [10] introduced a fusion model for emotion identification from voice and video based on the Dynamic Bayesian Network (DBN). They used a Berlin database for voice, and for face expression identification, they used a Cohn-Kanade database. In order to detect six primary emotions, a twofold cross-validation procedure was used.

The contribution of B. Schuller *et al.* is also commendable for using Hidden Markov Models (HMM) for emotion recognition [11]. They utilized supra-segmental modeling with systematic feature brute-forcing to analyze the 'mood' emotion in terms of valence and arousal.

4.4. EVALUATION

This section describes the most prevalent methods for evaluating the performance of an emotion detection system. The system performance varies with the nature of the database. The system performance is proportional to the environment and the population of data acquisition. The goodness criteria of a database depend upon varied samples recorded in various sessions with different subjects.

The system's performance is measured using an evaluation criterion, which must be calculated on the evaluation dataset. For multimodal information fusion, we may use three crucial assessment concepts:

- Types of errors
- Threshold criteria
- Performance criteria

4.4.1. Types of Errors

False Acceptance Rate (FAR) and False Reject Rate (FRR) are the criteria used to measure error.

4.4.1.1. False Acceptance Ratio

FAR is the ratio of the number of acceptance to the total number of imposters.

Equation 1 shows FAR.

$$FAR = \frac{NA}{NI} \quad (1)$$

4.4.1.2. False Reject Ratio

FRR is the ratio of rejects to the total number of instances. Equation 2 depicts FRR.

$$FRR = \frac{NR}{NC} \quad (2)$$

4.4.2. Threshold Criteria

A threshold criterion refers to a strategy to choose a threshold that is necessarily tuned to a development set. In order to choose an optimal threshold, we have to define a threshold criterion. The most commonly used criteria are Equal Error Rate (EER) and Weighted Error Rate (WER).

WER is defined as Equation 3:

$$\text{WER} = \alpha\text{FAR} + (1-\alpha)\ \text{FRR} \quad (3)$$

Where α ε (0, 1) balances between FAR and FRR.

The value of α will be 0.5, if the number of client and the number of imposter is equal. In this case:

$$\text{EET} = \frac{1}{2}(FAR + FRR) \quad (4)$$

4.4.3. Performance Criteria

The final performance of a system is measured using Half Total Error Rate (HTER). HTER is defined in Equation 5.

$$HTER = \frac{FAR+FRR}{2} \quad (5)$$

Another performance measure is gain ratio. Gain ratio refers to the gain obtained out of a fusion experiment. Suppose there are i = 1,2... N baseline systems.

$$\beta_{mean}\frac{mean_i(HTER_i)}{HTER_{com}} \quad \textbf{(6)}$$

$$\beta_{min}\frac{min_i(HTER_i)}{HTER_{com}} \quad \textbf{(7)}$$

Where HTERi,the HTER evaluation criterion as is associated to expert I and $HTER_{com}$ is the HTER associated with the combined system. β_{mean} and β_{min} are the proportion of the HTER of the fused expert with respect to the mean and the minimum HTER of the underlying experts i = 1,2,…., N.

4.4.4. Evaluation Metrics

We have covered the assessment measures for continuous emotion prediction in this part. The most generally used assessment metrics are mean absolute error (MAE), root mean squared error (RMSE) [6, 12].

4.4.4.1. Mean Absolute Error (MAE)

The MAE calculates the average of the absolute errors to evaluate the forecast and may be expressed as equation 4.8.

$$MAE = \frac{1}{n}\sum_{i=1}^{n}|f_i - y_i| = \frac{1}{n}\sum_{i=1}^{n}|e_i| \quad \textbf{(8)}$$

Where f_i is the prediction and y_i is the true value.

4.4.4.2. Mean Square Error (MSE)

The sum of the variance and the squared bias of the predictor is the Mean Square Error (MSE). It gives a score to the predictor based on the variance and bias. The RMSE is calculated as Equation 4.9.

$$RMSE = \sqrt{MSE} \quad \textbf{(9)}$$

Relative absolute error and root relative squared error are two further assessment measures.

4.4.5. ROC Curves

ROC stands for Receiver Operating Characteristic and measures the probability of usefulness of a test. The ROC curve can be drawn by plotting the TPR (or sensitivity) against FPR (or specificity). ROC analysis is inextricably linked to cost-benefit analysis in diagnostic decision-making.

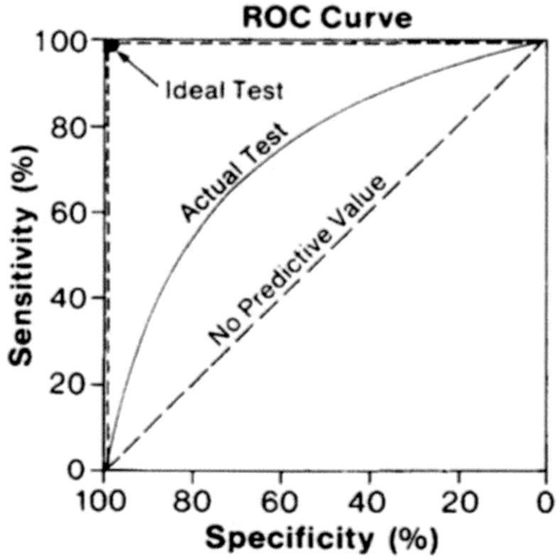

Fig. (4.1). ROC Curves for an Ideal Diagnostic Procedure *vs*. a Procedure that Produces No Useful Data.

The ideal condition for a ROC curve is a hundred percent sensitivity and specificity (Fig. **4.1**); however, an idle condition is not practically possible. As demonstrated in Fig. (**4.1**), the connection between sensitivity and specificity is linear when a diagnostic technique has no predictive value, and a random selection process makes the diagnosis. The observer determines the actual functioning point along this line. As this diagnostic process provides no usable information, increasing sensitivity by calling a higher number of positives will result in a commensurate fall in specificity [11]. ROC and PR curves are widely used to measure the performance of machine learning algorithms. There are a specified number of positive and negative instances in each dataset.

4.4.6. F1 Measure

The F1 measure (also known as F1score) is a metric for determining the correctness of a test. Precision (p) and Recall (r) are the two parameters used to calculate the F1 measure using equation 4.10 given below:

$$F_1 = 2.\frac{\text{precision.recall}}{\text{precision+recall}} \tag{10}$$

Precision (p) can be defined as the number of true positives over the number of true positives plus the number of false positives. Recall (r) is defined as the number of true positives over the number of true positives plus the number o false negatives. The F1 score may be considered a weighted average of accuracy and Recall, with the most outstanding value being one and the poorest being 0. The harmonic mean of accuracy and Recall is the classic F-measure or balanced F-score (F1 score).

CONCLUSION

This chapter describes information extraction and processing techniques reported in the literature. Various evaluation measures, such as types of error, F1 measures, Precision, Recall, ROC curves, *etc*. are also discussed in this chapter.

REFERENCES

[1] P. Nandwani, and R. Verma, "A review on sentiment analysis and emotion detection from text", *Social Network Analysis and Mining,* vol. 2021, pp. 1-19, 2021. [http://dx.doi.org/10.1007/s13278-021-00776-6]

[2] Z. Long, G. Liu, and X. Dai, "Extracting emotional features from ECG by using wavelet transform", *2010 International Conference on Biomedical Engineering and Computer Science,* 2010 [http://dx.doi.org/10.1109/ICBECS.2010.5462441]

[3] Dollár, and Piotr, "Behavior recognition via sparse spatio-temporal features", In: *2005 IEEE international workshop on visual surveillance and performance evaluation of tracking and surveillance.* IEEE, 2005.

[4] J. Kim, and E. André, "Emotion recognition based on physiological changes in music listening", *IEEE Trans. Pattern Anal. Mach. Intell.,* vol. 30, no. 12, pp. 2067-2083, 2008. [http://dx.doi.org/10.1109/TPAMI.2008.26] [PMID: 18988943]

[5] S. Koelstra, C. Muhl, M. Soleymani, Jong-Seok Lee, A. Yazdani, T. Ebrahimi, T. Pun, A. Nijholt, and I. Patras, "DEAP: A database for emotion analysis; using physiological signals", *IEEE Trans. Affect. Comput.,* vol. 3, no. 1, pp. 18-31, 2012. [http://dx.doi.org/10.1109/T-AFFC.2011.15]

[6] M.A. Nicolaou, H. Gunes, and M. Pantic, "Continuous prediction of spontaneous affect from multiple cues and modalities in valence-arousal space", *IEEE Trans. Affect. Comput.,* vol. 2, no. 2, pp. 92-105, 2011. [http://dx.doi.org/10.1109/T-AFFC.2011.9]

[7] Y. Wang, L. Guan, and A. Venetsanopoulos, *Kernel cross-modal factor analysis for information fusion with application to bimodal emotion recognition.* vol. 14. , 2012, no. 3, pp. 597-607.

[8] M. Paleari, R. Chellali, and B. Huet, "Features for multimodal emotion recognition: An extensive study", *Proc. CIS,* 2010pp. 90-95 [http://dx.doi.org/10.1109/ICCIS.2010.5518574]

[9] M. Mansoorizadeh, and N. Moghaddam Charkari, "Multimodal information fusion application to human emotion recognition from face and speech", *Multimedia Tools Appl.,* vol. 49, no. 2, pp. 277-297, 2010. [http://dx.doi.org/10.1007/s11042-009-0344-2]

[10] D. Datcu, and L.J. Rothkrantz, "The recognition of emotions from speech using gentleboost classifier: A comparison approach", *Proc. Int'l Conf. Computer Systems and Technologies,* vol. vol. 1, 2006pp.

1-6

[11] P. Sprawls, *Physical principles of medical imaging.,* pp. 69-82, 1993.

[12] I. Kanluan, M. Grimm, and K. Kroschel, "Audio-visual emotion recognition using an emotion space concept", *2008 16th European Signal Processing Conference. IEEE,* 2008

CHAPTER 5

Multimodal Affective Information Fusion

Abstract: The multimodal information can be assimilated at three levels 1) early fusion, 2) intermediate fusion, and 3) late fusion. Early fusion can be performed at the sensor or signal level. Intermediate fusion can be at the feature level, and late fusion may be done at the decision level. Apart from that, some more fusion techniques are rank-based, adaptive, *etc*. This chapter provides an extensive review of studies based on fusion and reported noticeable work herewith. Eventually, we discussed the challenges associated with multimodal fusion.

Keywords: Decision fusion, Feature fusion, Multi-modal fusion, Sensor fusion.

5.1. INTRODUCTION

Affective information plays a significant role in emotion recognition. The information acquired from multiple sources or modalities, such as audio, video, and text, is known as Multimodal information. Multimodal information fusion is described as merging information from many sources/modalities to produce superior performance than a single source/modality [1]. There have been several fusion categories mentioned in the literature. The fusion might happen at the signal, feature, or decision level. Early fusion occurs when the fusion is accomplished at the signal or feature level. Late fusion refers to fusion that occurs after a choice has been made. It is not required for distinct modalities to give complementary information in the fusion process, according to P. K. Atrey *et al.* [2], hence it is essential to know which modalities contribute the most. The appropriate number of modalities in the fusion process is a critical component.

5.2. MULTIMODAL INFORMATION FUSION

The early fusion integrates the information acquired from different modalities before applying learning models. Late fusion (also known as decision-level fusion) integrates the information acquired from the output of different algorithms or models. According to L. Hoste [3], Late fusion is based on the semantic information fusion obtained from different modalities. Each modality should be processed first, then integrated at the end to handle multimodal data. Several st-

Gyanendra K. Verma

udies [4 - 6] discussed fusion architectures and multimodal data processing. The data in multimodal processing is not necessarily mutually independent and, therefore, cannot be merged in a context-free fashion. However, the information must be processed in a combined space using a context-dependent model. The critical challenges in multimodal fusion are different feature formats. The dimensionality of joint feature space with temporal synchronization is another issue [4].

The two most significant aspects of multimodal information fusion are i) level of fusion and ii) the type of fusion. The fusion process must be synchronized. Time complexity and cost-effectiveness are the other performance factors. The fusion of two or more modalities must be done methodically. The primary difficulties in multimodal fusion are the number of modalities and information synchronization. The primary difficulties are a correlation between information collected from multiple modalities and the level at which the information is fused [7, 8]. During fusion, many modalities may not necessarily give supplementary information. As a result, it is critical to comprehend the contributions of each modality. The prime role of Multimodal information fusion is to combine data from different modalities/cues to eliminate ambiguity and uncertainty.

Information can be derived from various sources/modalities, such as text, images, and speech. The information can have low and high-level characteristics depending on the input source. The features are fused at either a low (feature fusion) or a high (decision level) level. The fusion techniques and associated works documented in the literature are also presented in this chapter.

5.2.1. Early Fusion

Information can be fused early, *i.e.*, at the sensor or signal level. A three-dimensional image, for example, can be created by fusing two or more two-dimensional images [9]. An example of early fusion is audio-visual information fusion, which integrates the audio and video information into a single feature vector. Dimensional reduction methods like principal component analysis or linear discriminate analysis can be used for dimensionality reduction. The two modalities are combined even before classification using Adaptive fusion. In Adaptive fusion, the weights are assigned to each modality, which is one of the essential advantages of early fusion. When we wish to give a modality greater weight, adaptive fusion comes in handy.

Numerous approaches have been reported in the literature to execute fusion, including Bayesian inference, Dempster–Shafer fusion, Maximum Entropy model, and Nave Bay's algorithms. Pitsikalis *et al.* [10] suggested a Bayesian inference-based technique integrating audio-visual information. They calculated the joint probability of integrated MFCC and texture analysis characteristics.

Mena and Malpica employed a Dempster–Shafer fusion technique for color picture segmentation [11]. For semantic multimedia indexing, Magalhaes and Ruger [12] employed the maximum entropy approach. For image retrieval, they integrated text and picture characteristics.

5.2.2. Intermediate Fusion

The drawback of the early fusion technique is its inability to deal with erroneous data that avoids explicit modeling of the various modalities. Early fusion methods suffer from relative dependability, fluctuations, and asynchrony. Such issue may be resolved by comparing the time instance feature to the time scale dimension of the relevant stream. As a result, by comparing previously seen data instances with current data transmitted *via* a working observation channel, one may create a statistical forecast with a derivable probability value for erroneous instances owing to sensor failures, *etc.*

Probabilistic graphical models are best suited for fusing numerous sources of data in this context [13]. Probabilistic inference also handles noisy features and missing feature values. A hierarchical HMM to identify facial expressions was presented by Cohen *et al.* [14]. The capability to fuse multiple sources of information of dynamic Bayesian networks and HMM variations was demonstrated by Minsky [15]. Carpenter R [16]. proposed a fusion approach to detect office activity and events in video utilizing audio and video signals.

5.2.3. Late Fusion

A multimodal system combines many modalities in order to conclude. It demands a standard framework for representing shared meaning across all modalities and a well-defined method for information assimilation [4]. Late fusion models typically employ distinct classifiers for each stream that are trained separately. The outcome is derived by fusing the outcome of individual classifiers. Only at the integration stage is the correspondence between the channels recognized. Late fusion has several clear advantages.

The inputs may be recognized independently, they do not have to coincide. The late fusion system employs classifiers that can be trained on a single data set but are scalable in terms of the number of modes and vocabulary. As with audio-visual recognition, we need to find a decent heuristic for extracting features from audio alone and restoring them using visual evidence [17]. Multimodal HCI is an example of an application in which sophisticated approaches and models for cross-modal information fusion are required to combine different modalities, such as audio and video. Several models are being presented to handle the problems of audio-visual fusion. However, it is still a universal challenge to integrate modalities optimally. The subsequent section discusses the study based on late fusion.

Aguilar *et al.* [18] suggested a rule-based and learning-based fusion technique for merging various cue scores using DET plots (face, fingerprint, and online signatures). The SVM classifier was used to obtain the combined score. They stated that a learning-based method beats a rule-based approach (with proper parameter selection).

Meyer *et al.* [19] suggested a decision-level fusion for isolated word recognition based on the study of time frames and phone segments. Individual judgments are obtained using HMM classifiers. The continuous voice recognition problem was then fused using Bayesian inference methods. Table **5.1** provides an overview of the fusion techniques regarding fusion methodology and modalities utilized for a number of applications. Table **5.2** provides an overview of the fusion techniques based on multiple physiological signals.

Singh *et al.* [20] introduced a fusion approach based on the D-S theory to improve the performance of fingerprint verification. They employed minutiae, ridge, finger code, and pore match scores. They claimed that fusion based on D-S theory outperforms individual techniques and cuts training time in half.

Beal *et al.* [21] presented graphical models for object tracking that combined audio and visual data. They used the graphical model to merge audio and video data. Model parameters were trained using the expectation-maximization approach from a multimedia sequence. Bay's rule was deployed to deduce the object trajectory from the data.

Gandetto *et al.* [22] presented an Artificial Neural Network fusion approach to recognize human behaviors in an environment. They used decision-level fusion to integrate the sensory data collected from a camera.

Table 5.1. Noticeable studies on fusion.

Fusion Level	Studies	Fusion Approach	Application
Feature	Pitsikalis *et al.* [10]	Bayesian	Speech recognition
	Mena and Malpica [11]	DS theory	Image Segmentation
	Magalha˜es and Ru¨ger [12]	Entropy Model	Semantic image indexing
	Nefian *et al.* [23]	DBN	Speech recognition
Decision	Aguilar *et al.* [18]	SVM	Semantic concept detection
	Meyer *et al.* [19]	Bayesian	Spoken digit recognition
	Beal *et al.* [21]	DBN	Object tracking
	Guironnet *et al.* [22]	DS theory	Human activity monitoring
Hybrid	Atrey *et al.* [2]	Bayesian	Sports video analysis
	Bredin and Chollet [24]	SVM	Biometric identification of talking face
	Zhu *et al.* [25]	SVM	Image classification
	Xie *et al.* [26]	DBN	Human tracking

Table 5.2. Noticeable studies on the fusion of multi-physiological signals.

Fusion	Studies	Fusion Approach	Features	Database
Feature level	Verma, Gyanendra K., *et al* ., 2014, [27]	Multiple kernel SVM and DWT	EEG + Peripheral	DEAP
Model-based	Dar, Muhammad Najam, *et al* ., 2017, [28]	Deep stacked AE, Bayesian model	EEG, EOG, EMG, ST, GSR, BVP, RESP	DEAP
Feature level	Hassan, Mohammad Mehedi, *et al* ., 2019, [29]	DBN and SVM	EDA, BVP, zEMG DBN, FGSVM Feature-level	DEAP
Decision level	Yang, Hao-Chun, and Chi-Chun Lee., 2019, [30]	AILE, SVM	EEG, ECG, EDA AILE-VAE	AMIGOS
Decision level	Li, Chao, *et al* ., 2020, [31]	Attention-based LSTM-RNNs, DNN	EEG, ECG, GSR	AMIGOS

5.3. LEVELS OF INFORMATION FUSION

Sanderson and Paliwal [32] classified fusion strategies into pre-classification and post-classification. Fusion before matching is referred to as pre-classification, whereas fusion after matching is called post-classification. Sensor level and feature level information fusion are subcategories of pre-classification schemes. In contrast, decision levels are subcategories of post-classification schemes. Pre-classification fusion is more challenging since the separate modality's classifiers may no longer be helpful. Fig. (**5.1**) depicts the various degrees of information fusion.

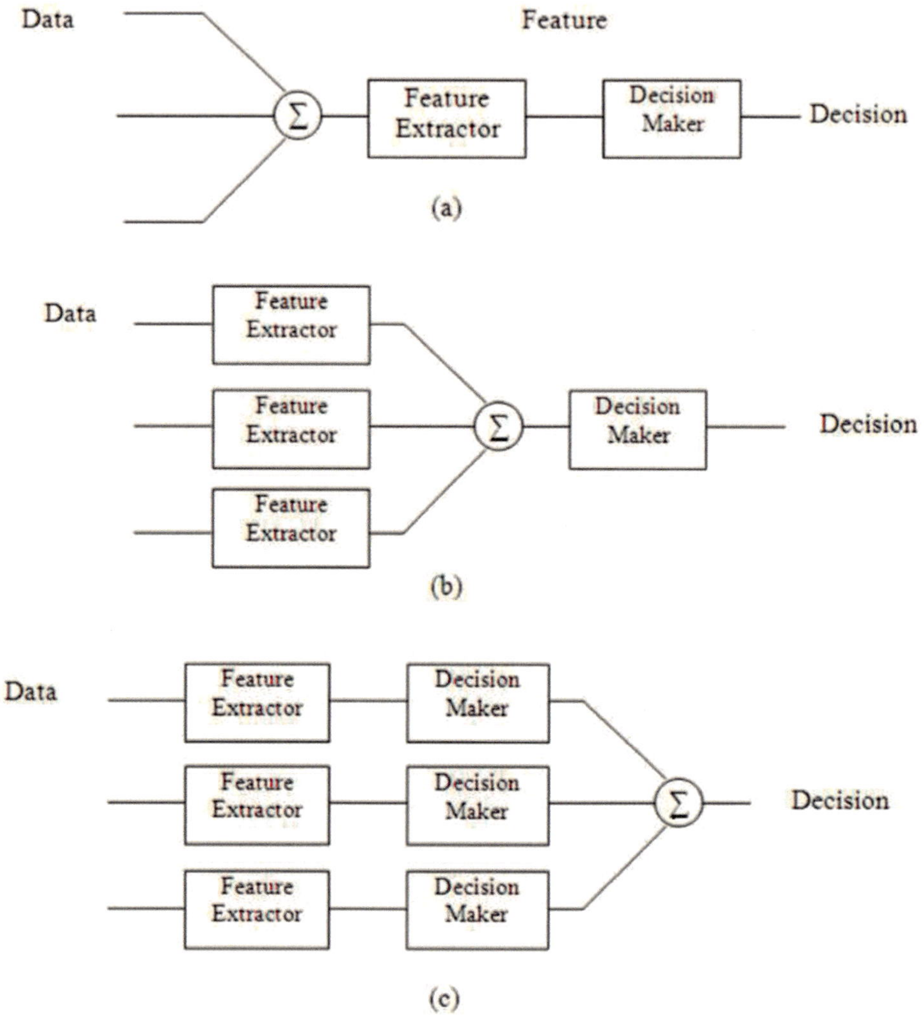

Fig. (5.1). A general architecture of information fusion **(a)** Signal level **(b)** Feature level **(c)** Decision level.

5.3.1. Sensor or Data-level Fusion

This fusion category combines raw data or data acquired from sensory (raw) data from several sources. The finest example of sensor-level fusion is creating a 3D picture from two 2D images. The type of sensors and information sources are two of the most critical concerns in sensor-level fusion. 2) Sensors' computational capability 3) topology, communication structure, and computing resources, and 4) system goals and optimization [33].

The prime advantage of sensor-level data fusion is system performance improvement. Other advantages are as follows:

I. Detection, tracking, and identification improvement.
II. Improved situational awareness and assessment.
III. Increased sturdiness.
IV. Coverage that is spatially and temporally extensive.
V. Reduced communication and computing costs and a faster reaction time.

5.3.2. Feature Level Fusion

Feature level fusion is achieved by extracting features from various modalities/sources individually, then combining them after normalization. The correlation between feature vectors that may improve the system performance can also be achieved using feature-level fusion. The challenges associated with feature-level fusion are feature normalization, feature transformation, and dimensionality reduction. The correlation across feature vectors and temporal synchronization among multiple modalities/ sources are also challenging tasks.

5.3.3. Decision-Level Fusion

The most popular fusion strategy is decision-level fusion, which integrates the classifiers' outputs. Each classifier's output can be merged using statistical methods, such as sum, 'AND,' 'OR', majority voting, and weighted majority voting A ranking or score may be created by applying statistical approaches to the output of individual classifiers. Score-level fusion combines that score and creates a new output that may be utilized to make decisions [34].

In rank-level fusion, the fusion is accomplished by combining the rankings produced by each modality/cue to arrive at a consensus rank.

5.4. MAJOR CHALLENGES IN INFORMATION FUSION

The following are the primary issues in information fusion:

1. How can one boost the resilience and reliability of the interface decision or input acquisition process by selecting signal attributes and using redundancy

among modalities?

2. What is the best approach to combine the information offered by each modality?

3. Regarding a given application, what is the relative relevance of different modalities?

4. How may source/channel coding be more efficient by utilizing redundancy among modalities?

CONCLUSION

A detailed review of various fusion strategies has been discussed in this chapter along with the pros and cons. The challenges associated with the fusion techniques are also discussed in this chapter.

REFERENCES

[1] G.K. Verma, *"Multi-algorithm fusion for speech emotion recognition", ACC-2011, Part III, CCIS 192.* Springer, 2011, pp. 452-459. a

[2] P.K. Atrey, M.A. Hossain, A. El Saddik, and M.S. Kankanhalli, "Multimodal fusion for multimedia analysis: a survey", *Multimedia Syst.,* vol. 16, no. 6, pp. 345-379, 2010. [http://dx.doi.org/10.1007/s00530-010-0182-0]

[3] L. Hoste, B. Dumas, and B. Signer, "Mudra: A unified multimodal interaction framework", *Proceedings of the 13th international conference on multimodal interfaces-ICMI '11,* 2011p. 97

[4] A. Jaimes, and N. Sebe, "Multimodal Human-Computer Interaction: A Survey", In: *Computer Vision and Image Understanding* vol. 108. Elsevier, 2007, pp. 116-134. [http://dx.doi.org/10.1016/j.cviu.2006.10.019]

[5] P.K. Atrey, M.S. Kankanhalli, and R. Jain, "Information assimilation framework for event detection in multimedia surveillance systems", *ACM Multimedia Syst. J.,* vol. 12, no. 3, pp. 239-253, 2006. [http://dx.doi.org/10.1007/s00530-006-0063-8]

[6] H.L. Chieu, and K. Y, "Query based event extraction along a timeline", *International ACM Conference on Research and Development in Information Retrieval,* 2004pp. 425-432 Sheffield

[7] N. Pfleger, "Context based multimodal fusion", *ACM International Conference on Multimodal Interfaces,* 2004pp. 265-272 State College

[8] S. Bengio, C. Marcel, S. Marcel, and J. Mariéthoz, "Confidence measures for multimodal identity verification", *Inf. Fusion,* vol. 3, no. 4, pp. 267-276, 2002. [http://dx.doi.org/10.1016/S1566-2535(02)00089-1]

[9] G. Cees, M. Snoek, M. Worring, and W.M. Smeulders, "Early versus late fusion in semantic video analysis", *Conf. on Multimedia,* 2005

[10] V. Pitsikalis, A. Katsamanis, G. Papandreou, and P. Maragos, *Adaptive multimodal fusion by uncertainty compensation.* INTERSPEECH, 2006. [http://dx.doi.org/10.21437/Interspeech.2006-616]

[11] J.B. Mena, and J. Malpica, ""Color image segmentation using the Dempster–Shafer theory of evidence for the fusion of texture", *Int. Arch. Photogram, Rem. Sens. Spatial Inform. Sci.,* vol. XXXIV, pp. 139-

144, 2003.

[12] J. Magalhaes, and S. Ruger, "Information-theoretic semantic multimedia indexing", *Int. Conf. on Image and Video Retrieval,* 2007pp. 619-626 Amsterdam

[13] N. Sebe, I. Cohenb, T. Geversa, and T.S. Huangc, "Multimodal Approaches for Emotion Recognition: A Survey", *Proc. of SPIE-IS&T Electronic Imaging,* vol. 5670, 2005pp. 56-67

[14] I. Cohen, N. Sebe, A. Garg, L.S. Chen, and T.S. Huang, "Facial expression recognition from video sequences: temporal and static modeling", *Comput. Vis. Image Underst.,* vol. 91, no. 1-2, pp. 160-187, 2003.
[http://dx.doi.org/10.1016/S1077-3142(03)00081-X]

[15] M. Minsky, A framework for representing knowledge.*The Psychology of Computer Vision.* McGraw-Hill: New York, 1975.

[16] R. Carpenter, *The Logic of Typed Feature Structures.* Cambridge University Press, 1992.
[http://dx.doi.org/10.1017/CBO9780511530098]

[17] J. Kittler, M. Hatef, R.P.W. Duin, and J. Matas, "On combining classifiers", *IEEE Trans. Pattern Anal. Mach. Intell.,* vol. 20, no. 3, pp. 226-239, 1998.
[http://dx.doi.org/10.1109/34.667881]

[18] J.F. Aguilar, J.O. Garcia, D.G. Romero, and J.G. Rodriguez, "A comparative evaluation of fusion strategies for multimodal biometric verification", *Int. Conf. on Video-Based Biometric Person Authentication VBPA 2003,* 2003pp. 830-837

[19] G.F. Meyer, J.B. Mulligan, and S.M. Wuerger, "Continuous audio–visual digit recognition using N-best decision fusion", *Inf. Fusion,* vol. 5, no. 2, pp. 91-101, 2004.
[http://dx.doi.org/10.1016/j.inffus.2003.07.001]

[20] R. Singh, M. Vatsa, A. Noore, and S.K. Singh, "DS theory based fingerprint classifier fusion with update rule to minimize training time", *IEICE Electron. Express,* vol. 3, no. 20, pp. 429-435, 2006.
[http://dx.doi.org/10.1587/elex.3.429]

[21] M.J. Beal, N. Jojic, and H. Attias, "A graphical model for audiovisual object tracking", *IEEE Trans. Pattern Anal. Mach. Intell.,* vol. 25, no. 7, pp. 828-836, 2003.
[http://dx.doi.org/10.1109/TPAMI.2003.1206512]

[22] M. Guironnet, D. Pellerin, and M. Rombaut, "Classification based on low-level feature fusion model", *The European Signal Processing Conference,* 2005 Antalya, Turkey

[23] A.V. Nefian, L. Liang, X. Pi, X. Liu, and K. Murphye, "Dynamic Bayesian networks for audiovisual speech recognition", *EURASIP J. Appl. Signal Process.,* vol. 11, pp. 1-15, 2002.

[24] H. Bredin, and G. Chollet, "Audiovisual speech synchrony measure: application to biometrics", *EURASIP J. Adv. Signal Process.,* vol. 2007, pp. 1-11, 2007.

[25] X. Zhu, X. Li, and S. Zhang, "Block-row sparse multiview multilabel learning for image classification", *IEEE Trans. Cybern.,* vol. 46, no. 2, pp. 450-461, 2016.
[http://dx.doi.org/10.1109/TCYB.2015.2403356] [PMID: 25730838]

[26] Z. Xie, and L. Guan, *Multimodal information fusion of audiovisual emotion recognition using novel information theoretic tools.* ICME, 2013.
[http://dx.doi.org/10.4018/ijmdem.2013100101]

[27] G.K. Verma, and U.S. Tiwary, "Multimodal fusion framework: A multiresolution approach for emotion classification and recognition from physiological signals", *Neuroimage,* vol. 102, no. Pt 1, pp. 162-172, 2014.
[http://dx.doi.org/10.1016/j.neuroimage.2013.11.007] [PMID: 24269801]

[28] Muhammad Najam Dar, "CNN and LSTM-based emotion charting using physiological signals", *Sensors,* vol. 20.16, p. 4551, 2020.
[http://dx.doi.org/10.3390/s20164551]

[29] M.M. Hassan, M.G.R. Alam, M.Z. Uddin, S. Huda, A. Almogren, and G. Fortino, "Human emotion recognition using deep belief network architecture", *Inf. Fusion,* vol. 51, pp. 10-18, 2019. [http://dx.doi.org/10.1016/j.inffus.2018.10.009]

[30] H-C. Yang, and C-C. Lee, "An attribute-invariant variational learning for emotion recognition using physiology", *ICASSP 2019-2019 IEEE International Conference on Acoustics, Speech and Signal Processing (ICASSP). IEEE,* 2019 [http://dx.doi.org/10.1109/ICASSP.2019.8683290]

[31] Chao Li, "Exploring temporal representations by leveraging attention-based bidirectional LSTM-RNNs for multi-modal emotion recognition", *Information Processing & Management,* vol. 57.3, p. 102185, 2020. [http://dx.doi.org/10.1016/j.ipm.2019.102185]

[32] C. Sanderson, and K.K. Paliwal, "Information fusion and person verification using speech and face information", *Research Paper IDIAP-RR 02-33, IDIAP,* 2002.

[33] P.K. Varshney, *Multisensory Data Fusion and Applications.* Syracuse University: Syracuse, NY, 2004.

[34] N. Poh, *Multimodal Information Fusion.* Multimodal Signal Processing, 2010. [http://dx.doi.org/10.1016/B978-0-12-374825-6.00017-4]

CHAPTER 6

Multimodal Fusion Framework and Multiresolution Analysis

Abstract: This chapter presents a multi-modal fusion framework for emotion recognition using multiresolution analysis. The proposed framework consists of three significant steps: (1) feature extraction and selection, (2) feature level fusion, and (3) mapping of emotions in three-dimensional VAD space. The proposed framework considers subject-independent features that can incorporate many more emotions. It is possible to handle many channel features, especially synchronous EEG channels and feature-level fusion works. This framework of representing emotions in 3D space can be extended for mapping emotion in three-dimensional spaces with three specific coordinates for a particular emotion. In addition to the fusion framework, we have explained multiresolution approaches, such as wavelet and curvelet transform, to classify and predict emotions.

Keywords: Curvelet transform, Emotion recognition, Wavelet transform.

6.1. INTRODUCTION

Multimodal fusion combines multiple cues that may act as complementary information to improve the system's performance. Several fusion approaches are reported in the literature; nonetheless, early, middle and late fusion are three primary categories. Before feeding into the learning phase, the features gathered from diverse modalities must be integrated into a single representation in an early fusion. Intermediate fusion can deal with insufficient data and asynchrony across distinct modalities. Decision-level fusion deals with semantic information as the decision is made by considering the outcome of different modalities after feature extraction. One of the essential criteria for multimodal data processing is that the data be processed individually before joining.

6.2. THE BENEFITS OF MULTIMODAL FEATURES

The challenging issues in multimodal fusion are 1) data types of modalities, 2) the synchronization of different types of modalities , and 3) the level of the fusion [1, 2]. The choice of fusion level may be easy for a similar type of data. For example,

Gyanendra K. Verma

if the two modalities are temporal, the fusion may be easy; however, if one is temporal and the other is special, fusion becomes challenging. The contribution of each modality is unique, and each fusion process does not need to enhance the system's performance.

Multiple modalities, such as text, picture, audio, and physiological inputs, can all have features extracted individually. The multimodal element not only adds to the information available but also has the potential to improve the system's performance. The following are some of the reasons for not relying on a single method of features:

6.2.1. Noise In Sensed Data

Sensor, channel, and modality-specific noise are the three forms of noise in sensed data. Sensor noise is the noise produced by the sensor. Each pixel of a camera sensor, for example, is made up of one or more light-sensitive photodiodes that convert incoming light into an electrical signal. The color value of the final image pixel represents the signal. Even if the same pixel were exposed to the same quantity of light numerous times, the resultant color value would not be equal. However, it would have a slight variance known as "noise."

Channel noise, on the other hand, is the result of the data transmission or medium deteriorating. Under slightly varied lighting conditions, for example, the same HCI modality may change. Person identification is perhaps the most well-known example. Under varied lighting circumstances, the same face looks different from two separate faces recorded under the same illumination conditions. Finally, modality-specific noise is noise induced by a disagreement between the acquired data and the standard interpretation of the modality.

6.2.2. Non-Universality

A system may not be able to get valuable data from only one modality. For example, complex emotions, such as pride, joy, excitement, sorrow, *etc*., cannot be identified by facial expressions only. Thus we must rely on other methods, such as physiological signals, to recognize complex emotions. Similarly, iris recognition biometrics may fail due to different eye conditions like long eyelashes, sloping eyelids, or certain eye pathologies issues. On the other hand, a face recognition system may nevertheless be a valuable biometric modality. While no one modality is ideal, combining them should provide more excellent user coverage, enhancing accessibility, particularly for the impaired.

6.2.3. Complementary Information

The information gained from the other modality can be utilized as a supplement. A single modality-based algorithm may fail if the input signal is lost or corrupted. A unimodal system may stop functioning in case of inputs from one modality interrupt. However, a multimodal system can continuously perform by taking inputs from other modalities. An object-tracking method based on visual modality works perfectly in the usual scenario. However, if the object occluded, it will stop tracking; in this instance, the voice modality may provide complementary information.

6.3. FEATURE LEVEL FUSION

Multimodal information fusion is the job of combining corresponding data from different modalities/cues in order to eliminate ambiguity and uncertainty. Depending on the applications, information can be acquired from various sources/modalities, such as text, pictures, and speech. The low and high-level features extracted from various modalities can be fused at either the feature level or a decision level.

Sensor level fusion combines raw data or data generated from several sources from sensory (raw) data. The finest example of sensor-level fusion is creating a 3D picture from two 2D images. The type of sensors and information sources are two essential concerns in sensor-level fusion. Other important characteristics for sensor level fusion are as follows [3]:

- Sensors' computational capability
- Topology, communication structure, computing resources, and
- System goals and optimization
- Improved detection, tracking, and identification are some of the benefits of sensor-level data fusion.
- Improved situational awareness and assessment
- Increased sturdiness
- Coverage that is both spatially and temporally extensive
- Reduced communication and computing costs, as well as a faster reaction time.

Feature level fusion is achieved by extracting features from several modalities/sources individually and then combining them after normalization. The benefit of feature-level fusion is that it can find the correlation between feature vectors, which can help the system perform better. The following parameters affect feature-level fusion.

1. Feature normalization

2. Feature transformation

3. Dimensionality reduction

4. The correlation across feature vectors

5. Temporal synchronization among multiple modalities/sources

The most popular fusion strategy is decision-level fusion, which integrates the classifiers' outputs. The classifier's output can be merged using statistical methods such as sum, 'AND', 'OR', majority voting, and weighted majority voting [4]. Score-level fusion combines the matching scores generated by several modalities to create a new output that may be utilized to make decisions [4]. In rank-level fusion, the fusion is accomplished by combining the rankings produced by each modality/cue to arrive at a consensus rank.

6.4. MULTIMODAL FEATURE-LEVEL FUSION

Multimodal feature-level fusion has been performed in this study by feature selection. The most discriminating features are chosen separately for each modality, and ii) feature fusion. A single feature vector is created by concatenating feature sets obtained from multiple information sources. The two feature vectors produced from modalities X and Y are $X = \{x_1, x_2, \ldots x_m\}$and $Y = \{y_1, y_2, \ldots y_n\}$. The goal is to create a new feature vector by combining the two.

For the merging of feature-level data from several modalities, we used the same technique. The many phases involved in feature-level fusion are outlined below.

6.4.1. Feature Normalization

The range and distribution of feature vectors collected from different modalities may differ. The goal of feature normalization is to normalize the range of each feature vector such that each feature vector's contribution is equal and comparable. Another advantage of normalizing is that it helps eliminate the problem of feature value outliers. Normalization methods include Z-score normalization, min-max normalization, *etc*. We experimented with many techniques and discovered that min-max normalization worked well.

Let x and x' represent a feature value before and after normalization. As seen in Equation **1**, the min-max approach computes x'. The min-max technique computesx' as shown in Equation **1**:

$$x' = \frac{x - min\,(F_x)}{\max\,(F_x) - \min(F_x)} \quad \textbf{(1)}$$

Where F_x is the function that generates x.

6.4.2. Feature Selection

Selecting features is critical since the most discriminating characteristics produce the best outcomes. The Analysis of Variance (ANOVA) approach is used to conduct feature selection on the feature values collected from diverse modalities. The Analysis of Variance (ANOVA) is used to sėlect characteristics acquired from diverse modalities. This method is based on whether the mean of two population samples should be comparable or not. Equation **2** may be used to get the F-ratio. The F-ratio can be calculated by Equation **2**:

$$F\text{-}ratio = \frac{\text{Variability among or between means}}{\text{Variability around or within the samples}} \quad \textbf{(2)}$$

$$\text{Variability among or between means} = \frac{\sum_{i=1}^{i=n}(\bar{x}_i - \bar{x})^2}{n-1}$$

Where n = number of samples

$\bar{x}_i$ = means of *ith* sample

$\bar{x}$ = mean of whole population

$$\text{Variability within or around sample} = \frac{\sum_{i=1}^{n}\sum_{j=1}^{k}(x_{i,j} - \bar{x}_i)^2}{\sum_{i=1}^{n}(k-1)}$$

Where $x_{i,j}$= *jth* element of *ith* sample

k = number of element in each sample.

$\bar{x}_i$ = mean of *ith* sample

6.4.3. Criteria For Feature Selection

A feature selection approach uses mutual information, correlation, or distance/similarity scores to pick features. Maximal relevance is one of the most prominent methods for achieving maximum reliance (Max-Relevance). The characteristic with the highest relevance to the target class is chosen using Max-Relevance. Relevance is often defined in correlation or mutual information. The latter is one of the most commonly used methods for defining variable reliance.

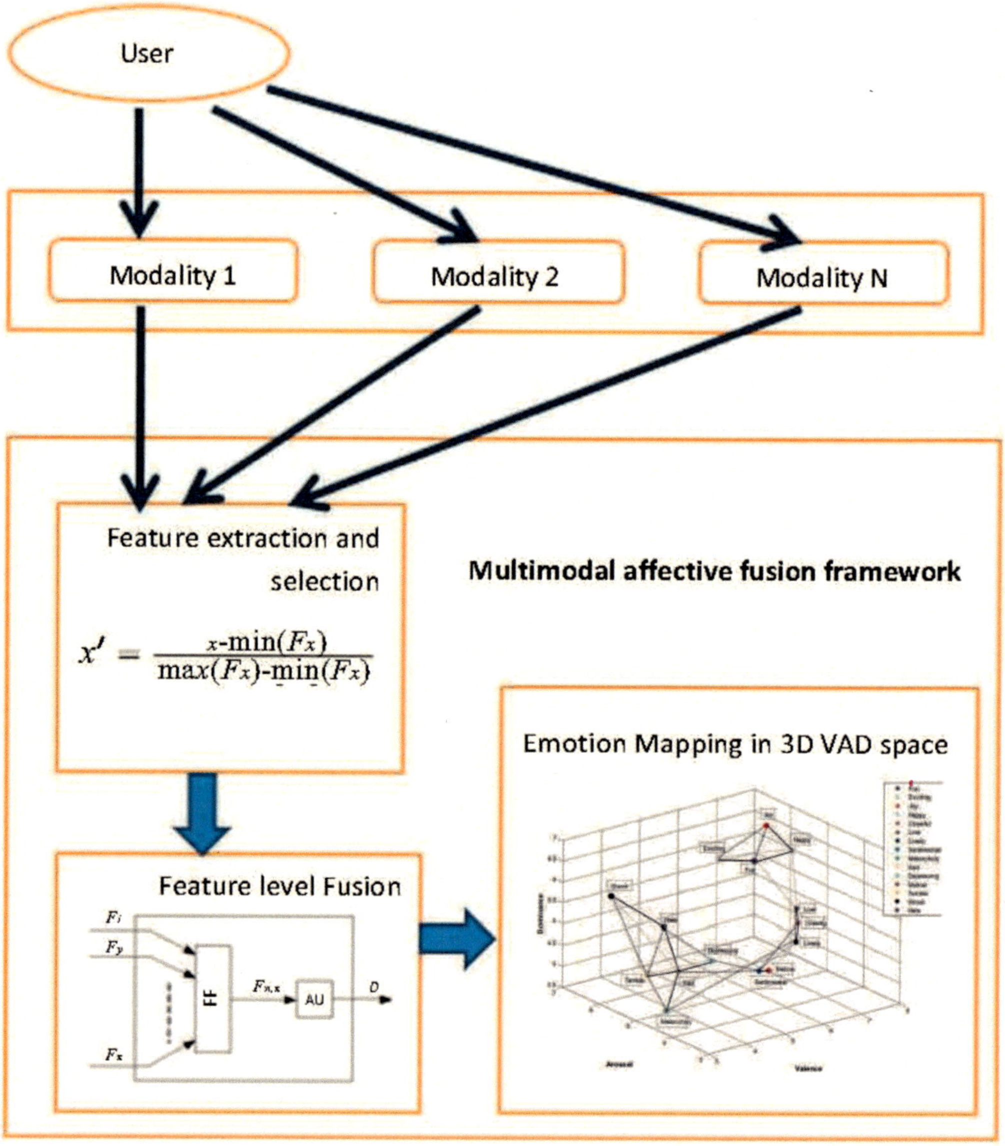

Fig. (6.1). A framework for continuous multimodal emotional integration that has been proposed.

6.5. MULTIMODAL FUSION FRAMEWORK

Audio, visual, and physiological inputs are utilized in this study, among other multimodal cues. The frontal face video frames taken from movies of various participants are used as visual cues. In contrast, physiological signals include EEG, EOG, EMG skin reaction, blood volume pressure, *etc*. We have looked into many areas of low and high-level fusion. At the feature level, the proposed approach is concerned with the best fusion of multimodal cues (audio, video, and physiological signals, for example). Fig. (**6.1**) depicts a fusion framework with all the stages outlined in detail.

6.5.1. Feature Extraction and Selection

The first phase in the proposed fusion paradigm is feature extraction, which involves extracting affluent and discriminating characteristics from emotional data. Several soft computing approaches, such as Principal Component Analysis (PCA), and Linear Discriminant Analysis (LDA), are reported in the literature to extract features from various modalities. Statistical measurements such as mean, variance, standard deviation, and entropy can be used to generate a final feature vector.

6.5.1.1. Extraction of Audio Features

Diverse speech aspects, such as mood, speaker audio, and both, represent different speech information. As a result, experts are interested in learning more about the speech characteristics of various emotions. Vocal tract, prosodic, and excitation source characteristics are the three types of speech features [5]. Short segments of voice signals are used to extract Vocal Tract characteristics. These properties represent the energy distribution for a variety of speech frequencies. Various studies employ various vocal tract elements and their combinations for emotion identification. T. Long [6] employed a mixture of Perceptual Linear Prediction (PLP), MFCC, and LPCC to distinguish emotions, such as angry, happy, sad, bored, and neutral, using the log frequency power coefficient (LFPC) vocal tract feature. As pitch has higher discriminating power than other prosodic variables, it is the most extensively employed prosodic feature for emotion identification. Aside from pitch, log energy is a popular metric for analyzing speaking styles and emotions.

6.5.1.2. Extraction of Video Features

The appearance of changes owing to lighting and position fluctuations complicates geometric feature-based face analysis. Spatio-temporal characteristics can be utilized to identify minor changes in a face. The interest spots in picture sequences are detected using Dollar's approach [7]. This approach is successfully used to identify minor changes in the spatial and temporal domains. The human action recognition community is most interested in detecting such minor changes. Multiresolution techniques may also be used to extract visual information from photographs.

6.5.1.3. Extraction of Peripheral Features from EEG

Physiological signals are vital for emotion, according to several emotion theories. Ekman established that a particular emotion might be linked to a specific physiological pattern. The frequency and amplitude of an EEG signal can be used to characterize it.

A band pass filter can be utilized to split the physiological signal into distinct frequency bands. Discrete Wavelet Transform is another approach for decomposing EEG signals into distinct frequency bands (DWT). Some examples of peripheral biosignals are:

- Galvanic Skin Response (GSR)
- Respiration amplitude,
- Electrocardiogram (ECG),
- Electromyograms (EMG),
- Electrooculogram (EOG),
- Electro Dermal Activity (EDA),
- Skin Conductance Response (SCR) and
- Skin temperature.

EDA and GSR are skin conductance measurements extensively utilized for automated emotion identification. According to J, GSR is a relatively reliable physiological marker of human arousal. Kim [8].

6.5.2. Dimension Reduction and Feature-level Fusion

Calculating the most discriminating qualities among several emotional features is a significant undertaking. Many dimension reduction methods are reported in the literature, including fisher discriminate analysis (FDA). Below is a basic overview of the FDA.

Let Φ is a non-linear projection to a particular feature space. The vector that optimizes Fisher's linear discriminate is presented as:

$$J(w) = \frac{w^T S_B^{\Phi} w}{w^T S_W^{\Phi} w} \quad (4)$$

Where now $w = f$ and $S_B^{\Phi} w$ and $S_W^{\Phi} w$ are the corresponding matrices in *f, i.e.*

$$S_B^{\Phi} w = (m_1^{\Phi} - m_2^{\Phi})(m_1^{\Phi} - m_2^{\Phi})^T \quad (5)$$

and

$$S_W^{\Phi} w = \sum_{i=1,2} \sum_{x \in x_i} (\Phi(x) - m_i^{\Phi})(\Phi(x) - m_i^{\Phi})^T) \quad (6)$$

With $m_i^{\Phi} = \frac{1}{l_i} \sum_{j=1}^{l_i} \Phi(x_j^i)$

6.5.3. Emotion Mapping to a 3D VAD Space

The suggested framework's last phase is mapping various emotions to the VAD space. The goal is to create an emotional mapping to the VAD space that allows each emotion to be represented in three dimensions. A learning algorithm can be used to carry out emotion mapping. We can employ Artificial Neural Networks (ANN) if the data uncertainty is considerable because each emotion has a valence, arousal, and dominance value. Each has a 3D point in VAD space, regardless of the labels employed.

SVR, Fuzzy k-NN classifiers, and a rule-based FLI approach may be used to map emotion characteristics in a 3D space. We opted SVR for mapping feature vectors into a continuous 3D valence-arousal-dominance space, rather than a classification into one set of class represented as $x_n^{(i)} \in [-1, +1] \subset \mathbb{R}$,i $\in$ {valence, arousal, dominance}.

A brief description of SVR is given below:

A function $f^{(i)}$ is to be selected, which maps the *m* emotion features $v = (v_1, .. v_m)^T \in \mathbb{R}^m$ to the 3D VAD space $f^{(i)} \in \mathbb{R}$

$$g^{(i)} = f^{(i)}(v) \quad (7)$$

To estimate the three emotion parameters separately, we required three SVR functions $i \in \{velence, arousal, dominance\}$

There is one solution to use a linear function, *i.e.*, a hyperplane in R^m

$$f(v) = \langle w(v) + b\rangle \quad \textbf{(8)}$$

Where $w \in \mathbb{R}^m$and $b \in \mathbb{R}$ b are the hyper parameters and $\langle\cdot\rangle$ Denotes the inner-product. A collection of N training instances $(v_n;\ x_n),\ n = 1, \dots N$ and $l(\eta)$ a loss function is penalise the distance between both the function's output $\hat{x}_n$ and truex_n,

$$l(\eta) = l(\hat{x}_n - x_n)$$

We have chosen the ε-insensitive loss function

$$l_\varepsilon(\eta) = \begin{cases} -\eta - \varepsilon for \eta < -\varepsilon \\ 0 \qquad for -\varepsilon \le \eta \le \varepsilon, \\ \eta - \varepsilon for \eta > \varepsilon \end{cases} \quad \textbf{(9)}$$

Within a wide margin around the real value, zero loss is assigned, while linear loss is assigned for bigger deviations. This loss function enables the hyper plane computation to ignore a large number of training samples. Support Vectors are the remaining samples. The problem may be phrased as follows. The structural risk is reduced with the low complexity of the function f.

$$minimize \frac{1}{2}\|w\|^2$$

$$subjectto \begin{cases} x_n - (\langle w, v_n\rangle + b) \le \varepsilon \\ (\langle w, v_n\rangle + b) - x_n \le \varepsilon \end{cases} \text{for n =1,2,...N(} \quad \textbf{(10)}$$

Allowing certain outliers is usual, and in our applications, very important. This may be accomplished by using *slack variables* ξ_n, ξ_n^* and a *soft margin parameter C*, which yields the following problem:

$$minimize \frac{1}{2}\|w\|^2 + C\sum_{n=1}^{N}(\xi_n + \xi_n^*)$$

$$subjectto \begin{cases} x_n - (\langle w, v_n\rangle + b) \le \varepsilon + \xi_n^* \\ (\langle w, v_n\rangle + b) - x_n \le \varepsilon + \xi_n \text{for n= 1,2,....N} \\ \xi_n, \xi_n^* \ge 0 \end{cases} \quad \textbf{(11)}$$

The dual Lagrange function, which involves the Lagrange Multipliers α_n, α_n^* as functions of the slack variables, can be used to rewrite this issue.

$$maximize -\frac{1}{2}\sum_{n,l=1}^{N}(\alpha_n^* - \alpha_n)(\alpha_l^* - \alpha_l)\langle v_n, v_l\rangle - \varepsilon\sum_{n=1}^{N}(\alpha_n^* + \alpha_n) + \sum_{n=1}^{N} x_n(\alpha_n^* - \alpha_n) \quad \textbf{(12)}$$

$$subjectto \begin{cases} \sum_{n=1}^{N}(\alpha_n^* - \alpha_n) = 0 \\ \alpha_n, \alpha_n^* \in \left[0, \frac{C}{N}\right] \end{cases}$$

The training samples vn only appear as inner products in this maximising task. One of the Lagrange conditions necessitates:

$$w = \sum_{n=1}^{N}(\alpha_n^* - \alpha_n)v_n \quad \textbf{(13)}$$

That is, we may fully represent as a linear combination of selected features, and the goal function *f* can be written as:

$$f(v) = \sum_{n=1}^{N}(\alpha_n^* - \alpha_n) < v_n, v > + b \quad \textbf{(14)}$$

While (14) is a useful formula that may be applied to any query characteristic.

Unknown emotion primitive values in vector **v0** with unknown emotion primitive values $x^{(i)}$ by evaluating $f(v = v_0)$.

The feature vectors only appear as inner products in (12) and (14), as is clear. A kernel function can be used to replace these inner products:

$$\langle V_n, V_l \rangle \rightarrow K(V_n, V_l) \quad \textbf{(15)}$$

The kernel technique is mathematically expressed in this replacement. It provides for efficient non-linear regression.

6.6. MULTIRESOLUTION ANALYSIS

The multiresolution analysis (MRA) examines the signal at several frequencies and resolutions. MRA approaches are generally mathematical frameworks for dissecting a signal into its elements. MRA approaches allow the discovery of efficient vector spaces capable of synthesizing the original signal from its deconstructed components. A subset of vectors in V defines vector spaces. v1, which span V v1, v2, ..., vn are linearly independent (which means every vector v in V can be generated by a linear combination of the subset elements). At high frequencies, MRA is designed to give good temporal resolution but poor frequency resolution.

On the other hand, it has strong frequency resolution at low frequencies but poor temporal resolution at higher frequencies. When the signal has high-frequency components for brief durations and low-frequency components for longer periods, this technique makes sense. Fortunately, this is a signal that frequently occurs in real-world applications. It has a low-frequency element all through the signal and a high-frequency element for a short time in the middle.

Wavelets are superior signal representations due to MRA. This is one of the reasons why wavelet transformations are currently being used in so many different applications. Wavelets have proven as a strong mathematical tool in a number of applications. Even though the time and frequency resolution limitations are caused by physical phenomena (the Heisenberg Uncertainty Principle), they persist independently of the transform employed. Any signal may be analyzed using a different multiresolution analysis technique (MRA). As with the STFT, not every spectral component is resolved equally.

The use of multiresolution analysis was motivated by the constraints of the Fourier Transform in constructing a frequency content of a signal using sine and cosine functions. When given a time-limited input, the Fourier Transform (FT) can supply the frequency content (with value and phase) required to synthesise a signal within its time limitations. When a signal's temporal restrictions are reduced, the signal's FT widens in the frequency response, making the transform more complex. To figure out which frequency elements are involved in the creation of a time-limited signal segment that is arbitrarily small. The Uncertainty Principle is a condition that MRA tries to address to the best of its ability.

In the last two decades, multiresolution methods, such as wavelet, curvelet, and contourlet transformations, have been effectively used to feature extraction. Although the wavelet transform can capture point discontinuities, it efficiently represents edge information [9]. Candes and Donoho [10] presented the curvelet transform, a multi-scale pyramid with various orientations and positions at each length scale, and needle-shaped components at microscopic scales. The curvelet transform is more complicated in terms of temporal complexity than the wavelet transform. The curvelet transform overcomes the drawbacks of the wavelet transform and is frequently used in computer vision applications [11].

6.6.1. Motivations for the use of Multiresolution Analysis

Wavelets and curvelets, for example, are commonly employed in Multiresolution Analysis (MRA) applications such as image segmentation, compression, and denoising. Wavelet Transforms provide numerous other advantages in study domains, such as biometrics, medical imaging, computer vision, affective computing, and multiresolution features.

- MRA [12] gives a concise representation of the signal's energy distribution in time and frequency.
- MRA can collect structural information based on several radial directions in the frequency domain. It allows for attaining features like directionality and anisotropy.

6.6.2. The Wavelet Transform

Wavelets are wave-like structures (mathematical tools) that decompose the signal into approximation and details and analyze the signal with different resolutions to simultaneously capture latent information in time and frequency domain.

Wavelet is a mathematical transformation function that separates data into distinct frequency components and analyses them with a varied resolution matched to its scale.

In signal analysis, a variety of functions may be applied to a signal to convert it into other formats that are more suited to different applications. The Fourier transform, which translates a signal from time vs. amplitude to frequency against amplitude, is the most often used function. This transformation is beneficial in various situations but is not time-based. Mathematicians devised the short-term Fourier transform to solve this challenge, which can convert a signal to frequency against time [11].

Unfortunately, this transformation has flaws, most notably the inability to achieve good resolutions for both high and low frequencies simultaneously. Therefore, how can a signal be transformed and altered while maintaining resolution across the transmission and being time-based? Wavelets are helpful in this situation.

Wavelets are the building blocks of the wavelet transform. Their ephemeral character distinguishes them from the Fourier transform's foundation. The wavelets have no high or low frequencies since they are flat and have a zero integral. Wavelets are dilations and translations of the mother wavelet, which is a single function. Equation 16 can be used to represent a one-dimensional wavelet mathematically.

$$\varphi_{s,d}(t) = \frac{1}{\sqrt{s}}\varphi(\frac{x-d}{s}) \qquad \textbf{(16)}$$

The scaling and translation, the two most important wavelet parameters, can be represented by s and d, respectively. The equation of CWT $W_g(s, d)$ of a signal g(t) can be given as:

$$W_g(s,d) = \int g(t)\varphi_s(t)dt \qquad \textbf{(17)}$$

6.6.3. The Curvelet Transform

Curvelets calculate coefficients by capturing data about an item at various sizes, positions, and orientations. Curvelet transformations, which have a greater accuracy rate, can be utilized. In the next subsections, the wavelet transform and the curvelet transform are explored. The curvelet transform is frequently utilized in many image processing techniques and astronomy because it overcomes the limits of the wavelet transform. In image processing, pattern recognition is a difficult task. To acquire a good result, a lot of calculation is required. At each resolution, the curvelet is a multi-scale pyramid with multiple orientations and placements and needle-shaped components at the finer scales. As this pyramid isn't common, curvelets have geometrical properties that set them apart from wavelets.

6.6.4. The Ridgelet Transform

The Ridgelet transform is closely related to the Radon and wavelet transforms. Ridgelets are an effective tool for discovering and displaying mono-dimensional singularities in 2D space. The Radon transforms [13] two-dimensional visuals with lines into the domain of possible line parameters. The lines in the image provide a peak situated at the right line parameters; this transform is employed in many line detection applications in image processing, object recognition, and pattern recognition.

$$R : L^2(R^2) \longrightarrow L^2([0, 2\pi]), L^2(R) \quad \textbf{(18)}$$

is defined as

$$Rf(\theta, t) = \iint f(x_1, x_2)\delta(\mathrm{x}_1 \cos\theta + \mathrm{x}_2 \sin\theta - t)dx_1 dx_2 \quad \textbf{(19)}$$

where δ is the Dirac delta.

The ridgelet coefficients Rf (a, b, θ) for an image *f* is given by:

$$R_f(a, b, \theta) = \int Rf(\theta, t)a^{1/2}\psi(t - b|a) \quad \textbf{(20)}$$

Where the variable t chasnges and the variable θ is fixed.

CONCLUSION

A multi-modal fusion framework has been presented to recognize emotion in this chapter. The multi-resolution analysis was applied to extract the features from the database. The proposed framework is capable of predicting a large number of emotions in three-dimensional Valence, Arousal, and Dominance space. Moreover, the framework can accommodate many features from various channels like audio, video, EEG, *etc*. The framework can be deployed for decision-level fusion with asynchronous data. In addition to the fusion framework, this study highlighted multi-resolution approaches, such as wavelet and curvelet transform to classify and predict emotions.

REFERENCES

[1] N. Pfleger, "Context based multimodal fusion", *ACM International Conference on Multimodal Interfaces,* 2004pp. 265-272 State College

[2] S. Bengio, C. Marcel, S. Marcel, and J. Mariéthoz, "Confidence measures for multimodal identity verification", *Inf. Fusion,* vol. 3, no. 4, pp. 267-276, 2002. [http://dx.doi.org/10.1016/S1566-2535(02)00089-1]

[3] P.K. Varshney, *Multisensory Data Fusion and Applications.* Syracuse University: Syracuse, NY, 2004.

[4] N. Poh, *Multimodal Information Fusion.* Multimodal Signal Processing, 2010. [http://dx.doi.org/10.1016/B978-0-12-374825-6.00017-4]

[5] Chien Shing Ooi, "A new approach of audio emotion recognition", *J. of Expert Systems with Applications,* vol. 41, no. 13, pp. 5858-5869, 2014. [http://dx.doi.org/10.1016/j.eswa.2014.03.026]

[6] Z. Long, G. Liu, and X. Dai, "Extracting emotional features from ECG by using wavelet transform", *International Conference on Biomedical Engineering and Computer Science,* 2010pp. 1-4 [http://dx.doi.org/10.1109/ICBECS.2010.5462441]

[7] P. Dollar, V. Rabaud, G. Cottrell, and S. Belongie, "Behaviors recognition via sparse spatio-temporal features", *VS-PETS,* vol. 2005, pp. 65-72, 2005.

[8] J. Kim, and E. André, "Emotion recognition based on physiological changes in music listening", *IEEE Trans. Pattern Anal. Mach. Intell.,* vol. 30, no. 12, pp. 2067-2083, 2008. [http://dx.doi.org/10.1109/TPAMI.2008.26] [PMID: 18988943]

[9] Q. Zhang, and H. Xiao, "Extracting regions of interest in biomedical images", *International Seminar on Future Biomedical Information Engineering,* 2008 [http://dx.doi.org/10.1109/FBIE.2008.8]

[10] E.J. Candes, and D.L. Donoho, "Continuous curvelet transform I: Resolution of the wavefront set", 2003.

[11] S. Prasad, G.K. Verma, B.K. Singh, and P. Kumar, "Basic handwritten character recognition from multi-lingual image dataset using multi-resolution and multidirectional transform", *Int. J. Wavelets Multiresolution Inf. Process.,* vol. 10, no. 5, 2012.1250046 [http://dx.doi.org/10.1142/S0219691312500464]

[12] G.K. Verma, "Multi-feature fusion for closed set text independent speaker identification", *5th Int. Conf. on Information Systems, Technology and Management (ICISTM 2011),* vol. 141, 2011pp. 170-179

[13] M. Miciak, "Character Recognition Using Radon Transformation and Principal Component Analysis in Postal Applications", *Proceedings of the International Multiconference on Computer Science and Information Technology,* 2008pp. 495-500 [http://dx.doi.org/10.1109/IMCSIT.2008.4747289]

CHAPTER 7

Emotion Recognition From Facial Expression In A Noisy Environment

Abstract: This study presents emotion recognition from facial expressions in a noisy environment. The challenges addressed in this study are noise in the images and illumination changes. Wavelets have been extensively used for noise reduction; therefore, we have applied wavelet and curvelet analysis from noisy images. The experiments are performed with different values of Gaussian noise (mean: 0.01, 0.03) and (variance: 0.01, 0.03). Similarly, for experimentation with illumination changes, we have considered different dynamic ranges (0.1, 0.9). Three benchmark databases, Cohn-Kanade, JAFFE, and In-house, are used for all experimentation. The five best machine learning algorithms are used for classification purposes. Experimental results show that SVM and MLP classifiers with wavelet and curvelet-based coefficients yield better results for emotion recognition. We can conclude that Wavelet coefficients-based features perform well, especially in the presence of Gaussian noise and illumination changes for facial expression recognition.

Keywords: Cohn-Kanade, Curvelet transform, Facial expression recognition, JAFFE, MLP, SVM, Wavelet transform.

7.1. INTRODUCTION

Emotions are essential for machines to make an intelligent decision. We are witnessing exponential growth in computing power, however, lacking robust algorithms that can enhance the intelligence of the machines. Emotions play a significant role in an intelligent behavior by machines at par with human beings [1, 2, 3, 4]. Emotions can be exhibited through various modes, such as facial expression, auditory expression, physiological expression, gesture, body language, sign language, *etc*. Facial expression is the most widely used modality among the above modalities due to quick presentation and recognition. Moreover, facial expressions are more accessible to acquire, process, and analyze than other modalities.

Multiresolution Analysis (MRA) proved useful in various applications, including medical imaging, satellite imaging, biometrics, *etc*.Wavelet and Curvelet transforms are two classical algorithms used for MRA. In [5, 6], wavelet

Gyanendra K. Verma

transform-based multiresolution analysis was performed. However, the application of MRA in a noisy environment is relatively new for emotion recognition.

Some of the research [7] works are based on applying multiple modalities rather than a single modality to analyze emotions. Mansoorizadeh *et al.* [8] proposed a multimodal fusion framework for human emotion recognition. Some of the work is based on curvelet analysis [9, 10]. Lee and Shih [11] presented contourlet analysis with regularized discriminate analysis for facial emotion recognition. Shan *et al.* [12] presented a facial expression recognition system using local binary patterns. M. Yeasin *et al.* [13] proposed an approach for the measurement of levels of interest from video for facial expression recognition.

Generally, raw images are degraded due to various phenomena such as varying lighting conditions, environmental effects, high/ low brightness, contrast, *etc*. Thus, facial expression recognition became more challenging in a noisy environment. This chapter deals with the recognition of facial expressions in a noisy environment. We have experimented with three benchmark databases to prove the proposed algorithm's usefulness and robustness. Various types of noise have been added with different mean and variance values. Then, the multiresolution approaches were applied to extract the most prominent features of noisy facial expression images. Getting the desired accuracy of the system in a noisy environment is still a challenge [14]. This chapter proposes multiresolution approaches based on wavelet and curvelet analysis to improve emotion recognition performance.

7.2. THE CHALLENGES IN FACIAL EMOTION RECOGNITION

The major challenge in facial expression recognition is noise and illumination change. The performance of most of the algorithms degraded due to the presence of these two parameters: 1) the presence of noise in facial expression and 2) varying illumination. We have recreated a noisy database by adding Gaussian white noise with different mean and variance values. At the same time, we have also modified the dynamic range of the test images by 0.1 to 0.9. The sample database images having different noise and illumination changes are shown in Fig. (**7.1**).

The images may be degraded during acquisition due to environmental conditions such as lighting, illumination, handshake, *etc*. The noise may also be added due to the sensor error during raw data acquisition. Many systems cannot preprocess or remove such added noise in the images. Therefore, a robust system is required to handle and analyze such noisy data efficiently. In an image, the edge information is degraded due to noise. It may happen even due to contrast reversals in some cases.

We have prepared the database for the experiments by adding Gaussian white noise in the images at different degrees. The values of mean and variance were kept in the range of 0.01- 0.03. For the first iteration of the experiment, the mean and variance values are set as 0.1 and 0.1. For the second test, the values are 0.03 and 0.03. Fig. (**7.2**) illustrates some sample images having additive noise. The research revealed that emotional signals could withstand noise-induced distortion. As all multiresolution approaches are inherently scale-invariant, we did not test for scale variation.

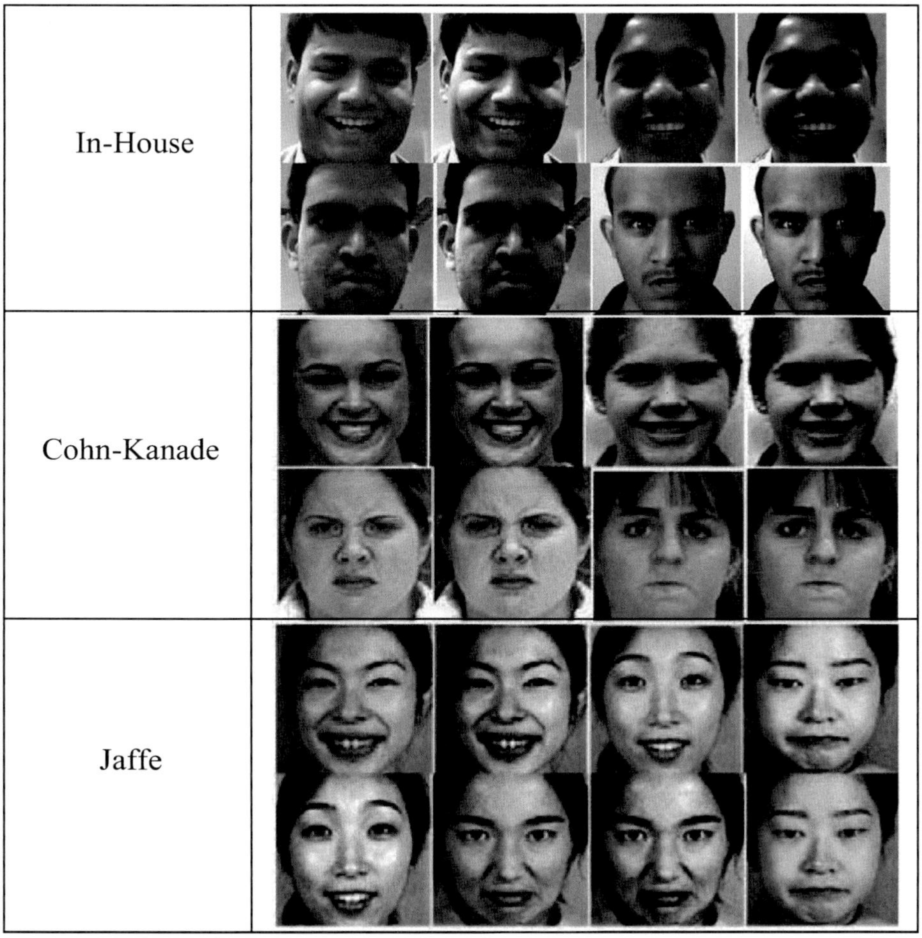

Fig. (7.1). Sample images with varying illumination conditions.

7.3. NOISE AND DYNAMIC RANGE IN DIGITAL IMAGES

Digital imaging records visual information from a charge-coupled device (CCD). A complimentary Metal-oxide Semiconductor (CMOS) sensor is placed at a focal length of the camera to measure the amount of light. The sensor is sensitive to light, as the brighter the light, the more electric charge is accumulated on the sensor. An array-based sensor's accuracy is proportional to the light arrived within the sensor and the amount of light gathered by the sensor to each pixel. This information is crucial for the quality of the image. CMOS sensors are efficient in capturing visual information compared to CCD sensors. There are various parameters contributing to image noise. Understanding these parameters would help find out the best digital imaging performance.

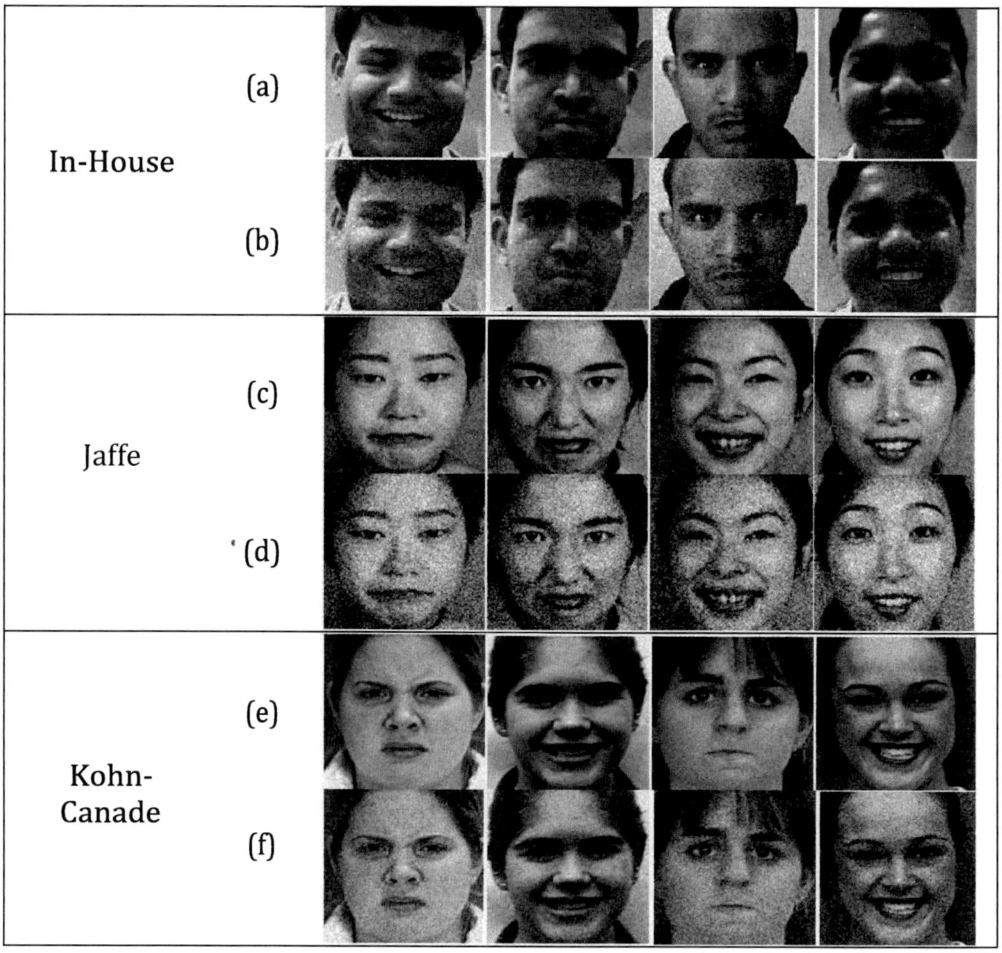

Fig. (7.2). Sample images with varying Gaussian noise; [Row a,c,e: (μ=0.01, $\sigma2$ = 0.01) | Row b, d, f; (μ=0.03, σ^2 = 0.03)].

7.3.1. Characteristic Sources Of Digital Image Noise

Digital image noise is unwanted data for digital imaging. There are various sources of digital image noise. A brief description of different sources of digital image noise is listed below.

7.3.1.1. Sensor Read Noise

Sensor read noise is created by converting each pixel into a standard read-out format. Before digitization, the charge is transformed to a voltage proportional to its number and amplified in the camera's Analogue to Digital Converter (ADC). As a result, each pixel experiences an identical read-out noise.

7.3.1.2. Pattern Noise

Any noise element that overcomes frame averaging is referred to as pattern noise. A signal recorded from the sensor while not exposed to light is known as fixed pattern noise. It restricts the strategy since camera identification from standard (non-dark) frames is difficult. The fixed pattern noise is a minor part of the overall pattern noise. Pixel non-uniformity noise, which is generated by varying susceptibility of pixels to light, is another essential component that survives processing better.

7.3.1.3. Thermal Noise

The photons are captured by the sensel in digital photography. Then, proportionate to the number of photons, these photons are transformed into electrical charges. Thermal agitation of electrons yields electrons that are distinguishable from those released by photon (light) absorption. As a result, the photon count reflected by the raw data is distorted. As the electrons are discharged steadily, thermal noise grows with time.

7.3.1.4. Pixel Response Non-uniformity (PRNU)

Pixel response non-uniformity (PRNU): Under different noise situations, such as photon noise and read-out noise, the pixel's effectiveness in catching and counting photons might vary. Due to the non-uniformity of pixel response, there is always a fluctuation in raw counts.

7.3.1.5. Quantization Rrror

When the sensor converts the analog voltage signal into a raw value, it is reduced to a close integer value, which causes a quantization error. The raw number significantly misrepresents the actual signal due to this rounding-off. Quantization noise is the noise added to a signal due to a quantization error. In practice, it simply provides a small quantity of noise [15].

7.4. THE DATABASE

To assess the emotions of frontal facial photographs, we employed JAFFE, Cohn-Kanade, and an in-house database. The first two emotion databases are industry standards that have been successfully implemented in various applications. On the other hand, the third database is an in-house database created at our laboratory. Fig. (**7.3**) show glimpses of all three databases.

7.4.1. Cohn-Kanade Database

The visual sequences from neutral to stimulated are digitized into 640 490 pixels with 8-bit grayscale precision in the Cohn-Kanade database [16]. Three hundred twenty picture sequences were chosen from 96 people for studies, as in [17] and [18]. For each series, the neutral face and three peak frames were utilized for prototype expression identification, yielding 1409 pictures.

7.4.2. JAFFE Database

We used the JAFFE (Japanese Female Facial Expression) database [19] as a baseline for many emotion investigations. Ten Japanese girls with seven facial emotions are included in the database: neutral, pleased, furious, disgusted, fearful, sad, and surprised. For each expression, each female gets two to four examples. There are 213 grayscale face expression pictures, every 256×256 pixels in size.

7.4.3. In-House Database

There are 213 photos of various facial expressions in the in-house database. There are 213 grayscale face expression pictures totaling 256×256 pixels in size. Furthermore, our in-house dataset is available for review and experimentation online at [sites.google.com/site/cjidataset/].

7.5. EXPERIMENTS WITH THE PROPOSED FRAMEWORK

A data processing tool, Mazda analyzed facial expression images. Mazda is an efficient analyzer to extract features like texture, histogram, gradients, run-length metrics, and co-occurrence matrics-based features. Wavelet analysis may also be performed using Mazda.

We have considered six classes (fear, happiness, dad, disgust, anger, and surprise) of emotions for the experimentation. The database utilized is JAFFE, Cohn-Kanade, and the In-house database compiled by us in laboratory conditions. The above databases have been successfully used in various applications, including [12, 13, 20, 21].

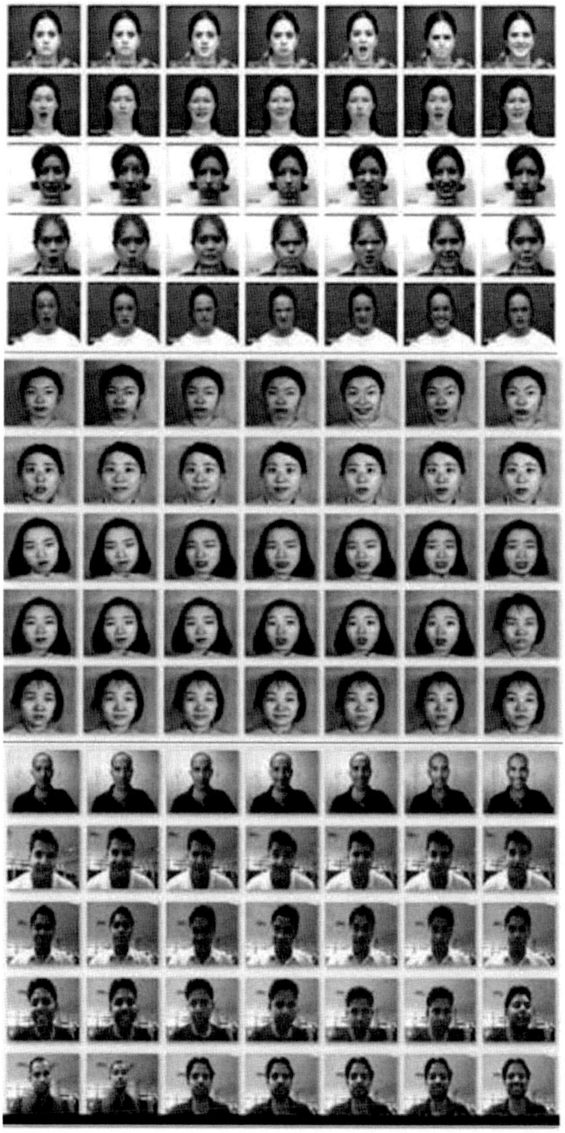

Fig. (7.3). Sample images form **(a)** Cohn-Kanade **(b)** JAFFE and **(c)** In-House database.

7.5.1. Image Pre-Processing

Preprocessing is a crucial step in removing the noise and error in the raw signal. Preprocessing techniques include database normalization, rescaling, removal of DC artifacts, removal of zero error, *etc*. To adjust the ranges of grey level values, we did picture normalization. In digital signal processing, it is referred to as contrast stretching or dynamic range extension. A fixed value decreases each pixel's intensity from the corresponding value. 0 to 130 is the new range to normalize a picture from a grayscale value to the required value. The pixel intensities are multiplied by a factor of 255/130, resulting in a new range of 0 to 255. Dimensional shifts from Xj to Yj, j = 1; 2; a change in the image's sample rate in each dimension is normalization's outcome.

7.5.2. Feature Extraction

Any emotion recognition system's success is proportionally proportional to the most discriminating features extracted from input data. A good feature's significant characteristics are high inter-class and low intra-class similarity. Fig. (**7.4**) shows how to do a curvelet analysis on a picture. We captured thirty photos of several subjects expressing various moods. We chose the lips, eyebrows, chin, and other facial features as a zone of interest since they are the most discerning in expressing emotion (ROI). We graded characteristics based on inter-class separability due to many features. We computed the highest discriminating characteristics among distinct emotion classes using fisher discriminate analysis. The discrimination percentage of features is then used to rank them.

7.5.3. Feature Matching

The classification was performed with the five best classifiers:

- Support Vector Machine (SVM)
- Multilayer Perception (MLP),
- K-Nearest Neighbor (KNN),
- K* (K-Star) and
- Meta multiclass (MMC)

All characteristics used for classification were standardized to a range of [0, 1] using min-max normalization prior to testing. A separating hyperplane defines SVM, which is a discriminative supervised classifier. In SVM, we prefer to use larger cost parameter values (C = 200 and above) to reduce the misclassification rate [22, 23]. KNN is an instance-based non-parametric learning method that gives a class membership to an input item based on the votes of its k nearest neighbors.

MLP is a multi-layered feed-forward neural network that adapts to a set of inputs by learning from them. Each node (neuron) in the network has its non-linear activation function.

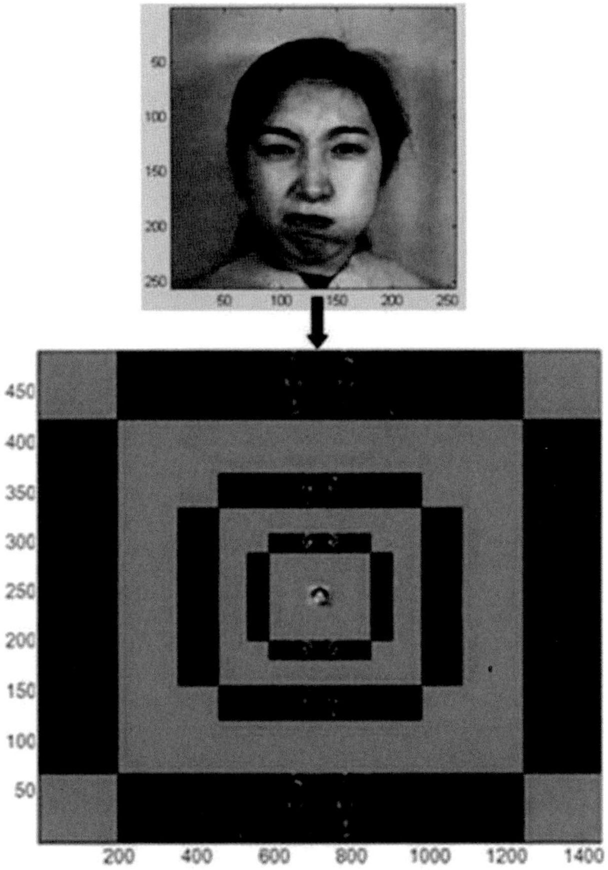

Fig. (7.4). Curvelet analysis with an image of the JAFFE database.

K* is an instance-based classifier, which means that the class of related training examples decides the class of a test instance, as defined by a similarity function [24].

The Meta Multiclass classifier can handle multiclass classifications in a cost-sensitive classification setting. It can also use error-correcting output codes to improve accuracy [25]. To validate the user-independent categorization performance, we employed a 10-fold cross-validation approach. The cross-validation approach assures that every dataset instance has an equal probability of appearing in both the training and testing sets. The 10-fold cross-validation method splits the data into ten pieces and trains each one ten times, with a new chunk serving as the holdout set each time.

The C parameter for the SVM classifier is empirically set to 200 with a round-off error of 1.0 e–12 using the RBF kernel. The tolerance parameter has been set at 0.001. The learning rate for MLP is 0.3, the number of epochs is 500, and the threshold (for the number of consecutive mistakes) is 20. All tests were run on a 64-bit Intel i5 CPU (2.40 GHz) with 4 GB RAM using MATLAB8.1.0 (R2013a).

7.6. RESULTS AND DISCUSSIONS

Wavelet and curvelet analyses were carried out with various resolutions and scales. Initially, results are evaluated using several wavelet families/functions (*e.g.*, bior2.4, db4, db10, dmey, *etc.*) and a curvelet transforms variation (*e.g.*, usfft, wrapper curvelet, wrapper wavelet). We utilized the dmey (Meyer) function to extract features and generate a feature vector since it outperforms. Similarly, a wrapper curvelet was utilized while extracting features using the curvelet transform. The comparative performances for different wavelet and curvelet functions are shown in Figs. **(7.5** and **7.6**).

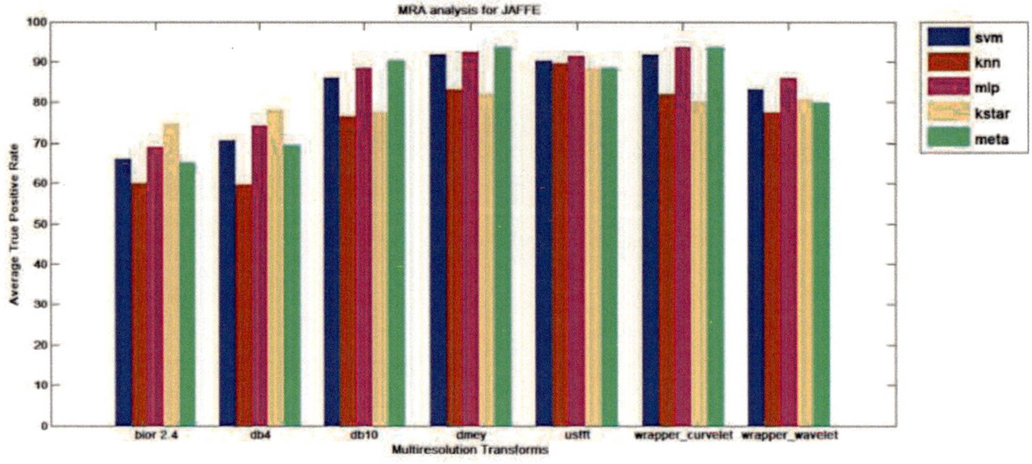

Fig. (7.5). Performance graph with Wavelet and Curvelets (JAFFE database).

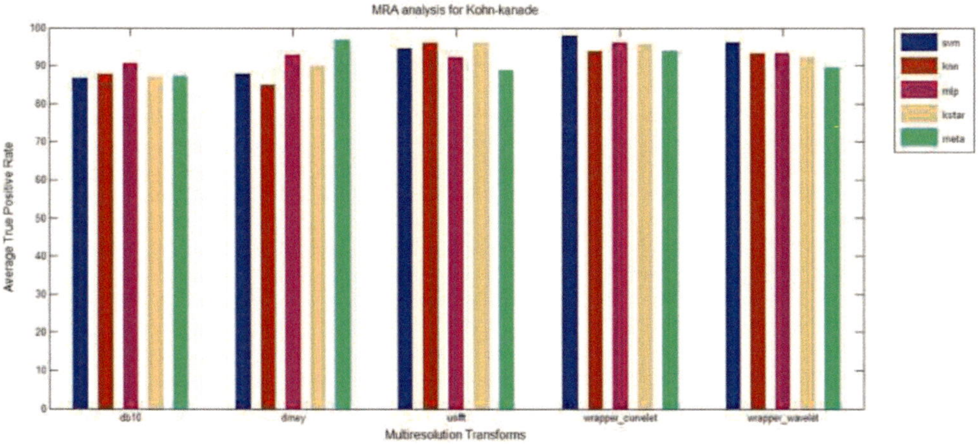

Fig. (7.6). Performance graph with Wavelet and Curvelets (Cohn-Kanade database).

The results are based on wavelet families such as "dBoir," "Daubechies," and "dmey," among others. Several Curvelet transformations, such as usfft, wrapper curvelet, and wrapper wavelet, were utilized for the analysis. However, the results for wavelet "dmey" at level 6 and wrapper curvelet are shown for the databases indicated above. A wavelet function on a 256×256 grayscale image took between 250–300 ms, and a curvelet function on a grayscale image with an identical resolution took between 300–400 milliseconds. (Figs. **7.7, 7.8, 7.9, 7.10**), and Tables **7.1** and **7.2** for five distinct classifiers demonstrate the accuracies in terms of True Positive Rate (TPR), False Positive Rate (FPR), Precision, Recall, F-measure, Matthews Correlation Coefficient (MCC), Receiver Operating Characteristic area (ROC area), and Precision-Recall Curve.

It can be seen from the performance (Figs. **7.7, 7.8, 7.9, 7.10**) and Tables **7.1** & **7.2** that MLP and SVM outperformed compared to other classifiers. Fig. (**7.11**) shows the classification accuracies for wavelet and curvelet analysis. The curvelet analysis provides the best results in all database categories with an SVM classissfier. The confusion matrices for six classes of emotions (for five classifiers) are presented in Table **7.3** and Table **7.4**.

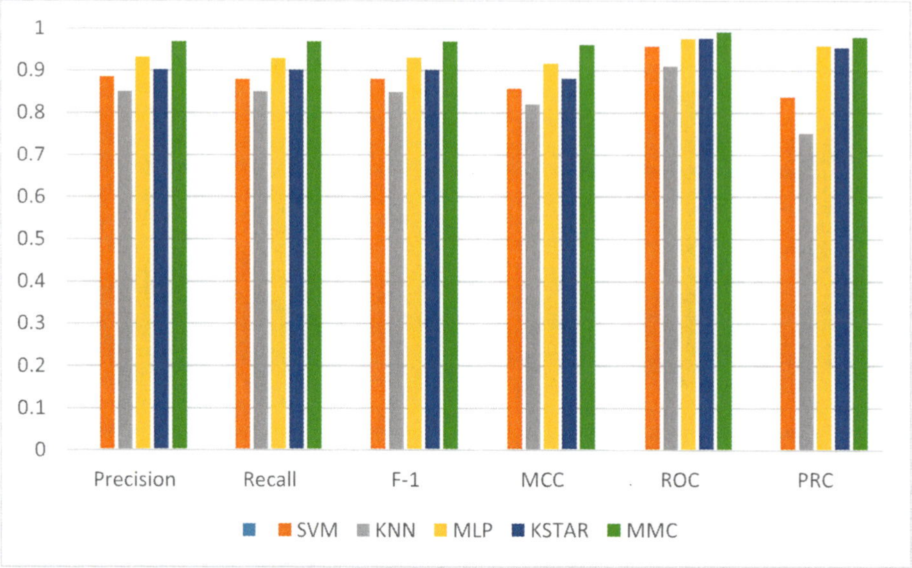

Fig. (7.7). Performance with Kohn-Canade database using wavelet (dmay, 6).

Fig. (7.8). Performance with Kohn-Canade database using wrapper_curvelet.

7.7. RESULTS UNDER ILLUMINATION CHANGES

The visual components of a facial expression are changed by illumination, making it challenging to construct a reliable emotion analyzer. Shadows, unsynchronized adjustments to fast intensity changes during picture capture, and other factors can cause illumination variations. Shifts in the placement and form of shadows, reversal of visual gradients, and other effects are occasionally caused by changes in illumination. Fig. (**7.12**) depicts the change in lighting as a function of dynamic range (0.1, 0.9).

7.8. RESULTS UNDER GAUSSIAN NOISE

The experiments were conducted with different parameters such as decomposition level and the number of coefficients, to yield the feature vector. Figs. (**7.13** and **7.14**) show the system's performance under different Gaussian noises. It can be concluded that the optimum performance is achieved using multiresolution algorithms. From Figs. (**7.13** and **7.14**), it can also be concluded that the Curvelet outperforms under different Gaussian noise conditions. The experimental results show that MRA outperforms under noise conditions. A comparative study is given to investigate the performance of different algorithms with different databases (in-house, Cohn-Kanade, and JAFFE databases).

7.8.1. Comparison with other Strategies

Accuracy comparisons with other systems based on Cohn-Kanade and JAFFE databases are given in Tables **7.5** and **7.6**, respectively. It is observed that the performance of our system is 97.8% for Cohn-Kanade and 93.4% for the JAFFE database, which performed better compared to the performance of other systems, as shown in Tables **7.5** and **7.6**.

Table 7.1. Performance with In-House database using wavelet (dmay,6).

Classifier	TP Rate	FP	Precision	Recall	F-1	MCC	ROC	PRC
SVM	0.745	0.055	0.725	0.745	0.733	0.682	0.866	0.669
KNN	0.531	0.121	0.507	0.531	0.516	0.405	0.702	0.391
MLP	0.786	0.05	0.765	0.786	0.774	0.73	0.915	0.807
KSTAR	0.538	0.125	0.509	0.538	0.517	0.408	0.833	0.598
MMC	0.814	0.044	0.809	0.814	0.807	0.769	0.911	0.819

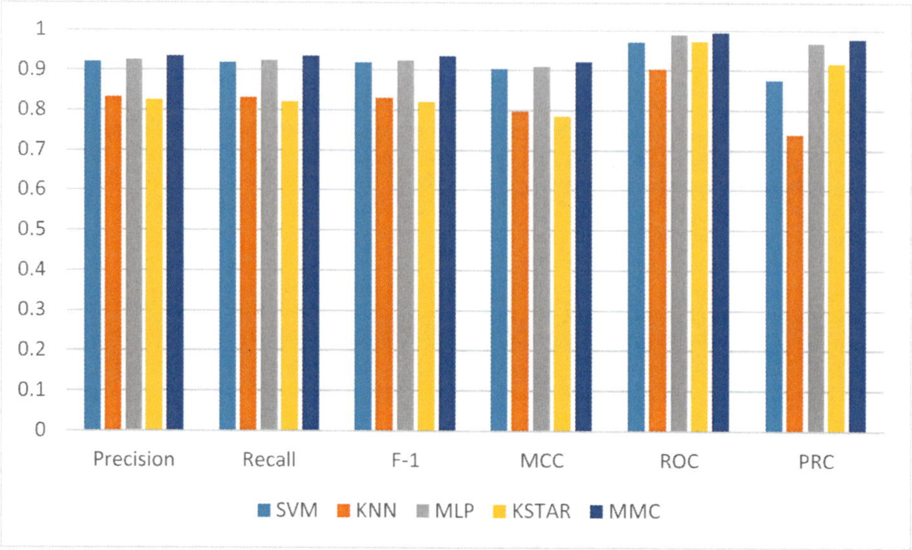

Fig. (7.9). Performance with JAFFE database using wavelet. (dmay, 6).

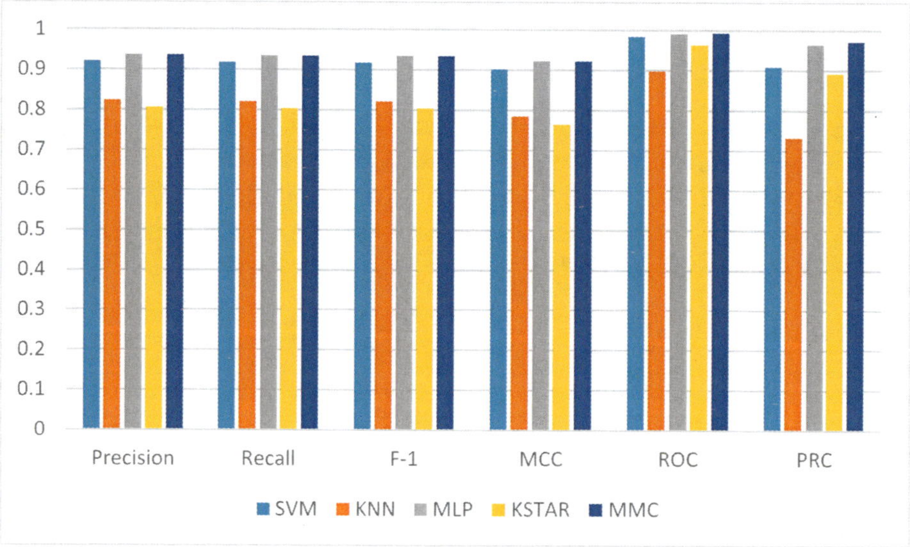

Fig. (7.10). Performance with JAFFE database using wrapper_curvelet.

Table 7.2. Performance with In-House database using wrapper_curvelet.

Classifier	TP	FP	Precision	Recall	F-1	MCC	ROC	PRC
SVM	0.855	0.037	0.826	0.855	0.84	0.809	0.916	0.786
KNN	0.6	0.126	0.634	0.6	0.595	0.493	0.734	0.451
MLP	0.862	0.035	0.826	0.862	0.843	0.815	0.942	0.886
KSTAR	0.586	0.141	0.61	0.586	0.575	0.472	0.844	0.648
MMC	0.807	0.053	0.786	0.807	0.793	0.753	0.937	0.856

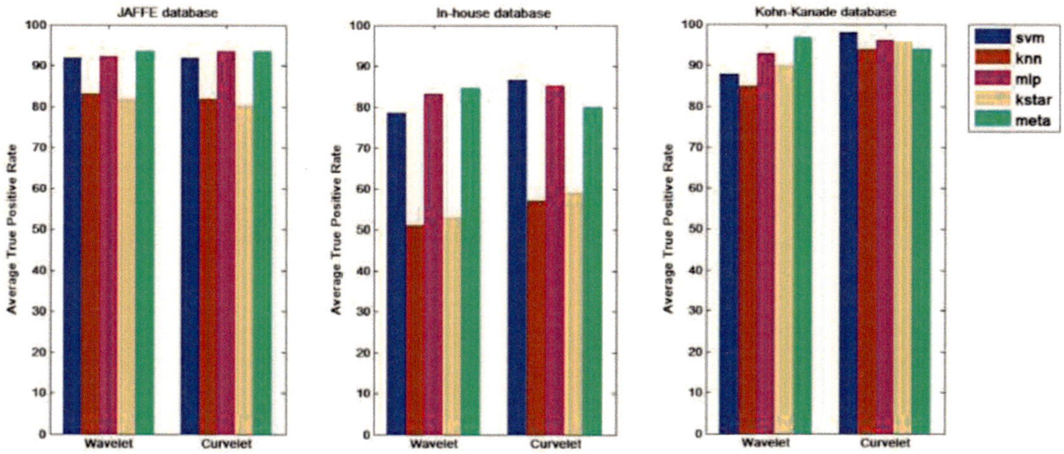

Fig. (7.11). Average TP rate graph with different classifiers for different databases.

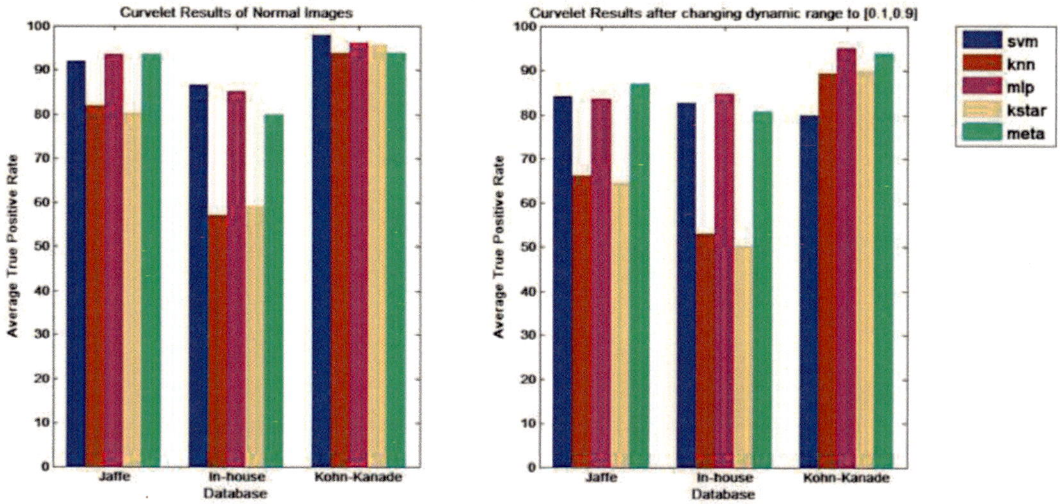

Fig. (7.12). Effect of illumination changes with dynamic range on average TP rate.

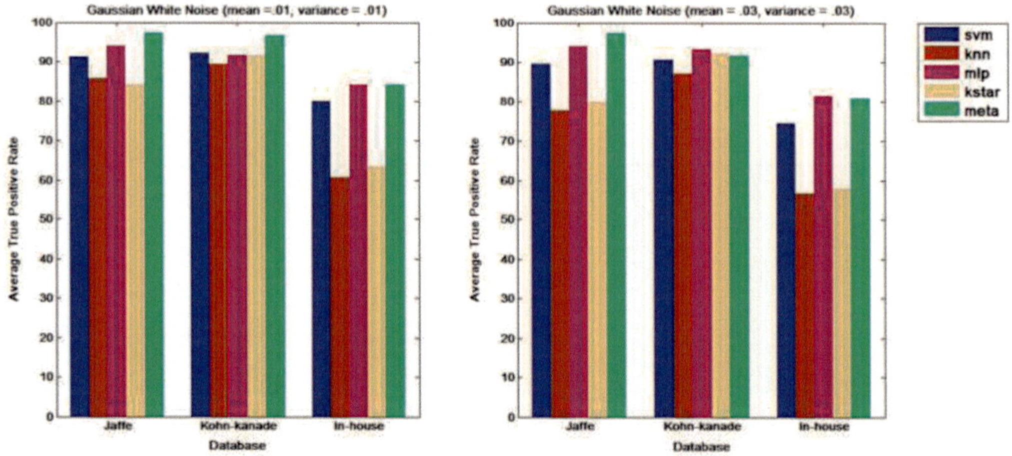

Fig. (7.13). Accuracy with Gaussian White Noise using Wavelet.

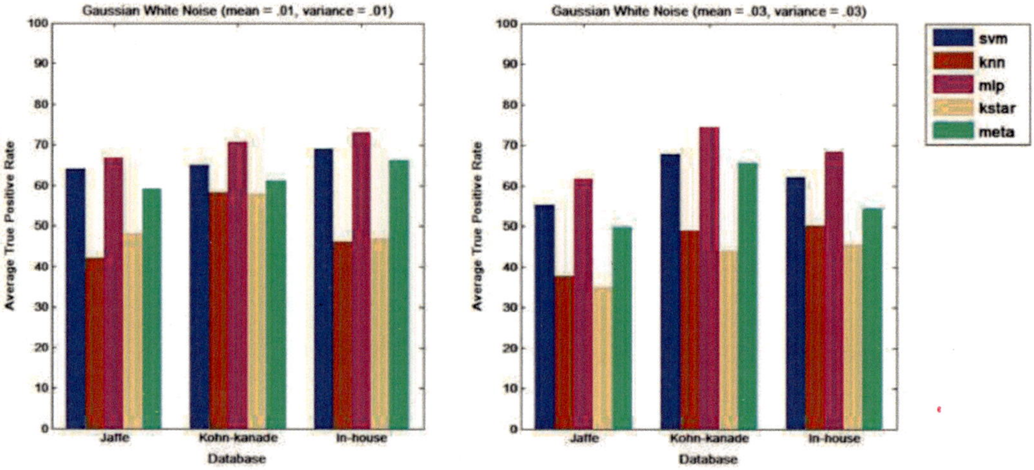

Fig. (7.14). Accuracy with Gaussian White Noise using Curvelet.

Table 7.3. Confusion metrics for JAFFE database using wavelet analysis.

-	A	D	F	H	S	Su
A	96.66	0	0	0	0	3.33
D	0	96.55	0	3.44	0	0
F	0	3.12	93.75	0	0	3.12
H	0	0	0	96.77	0	3.22
S	0	6.45	3.22	0	87.09	3.22
Su	0	6.66	10	3.33	0	80

(SVM)

(Table 7.3) cont.....

-	A	D	F	H	S	Su
A	83.33	10	3.33	3.33	0	0
D	3.44	82.75	6.89	3.44	0	3.44
F	3.12	3.12	84.37	0	0	9.37
H	0	0	0	87.09	12.90	0
S	6.45	3.22	6.45	9.67	74.19	0
Su	0	0	10	3.33	0	86.66

(KNN)

-	A	D	F	H	S	Su
A	100	0	0	0	0	0
D	3.44	86.20	3.44	6.89	0	0
F	0	0	90.62	0	3.12	6.25
H	0	0	3.22	96.77	0	0
S	0	0	3.226	0	96.77	0
Su	0	6.66	10	0	0	83.33

(MLP)

-	A	D	F	H	S	Su
A	83.33	6.66	6.66	3.33	0	0
D	3.44	89.65	3.44	0	3.44	0
F	3.12	3.12	78.12	0	9.37	6.25
H	0	0	3.22	90.32	6.45	0
S	12.90	0	9.67	0	77.41	0
Su	3.33	0	10	10	3.33	73.33

(KSTAR)

-	A	D	F	H	S	Su
A	93.33	3.33	0	3.33	0	0
D	3.44	86.20	3.44	0	3.44	3.44
F	0	0	96.87	0	0	3.12

(Table 7.3) cont.....

H	0	0	0	100	0	0
S	3.22	0	0	0	93.54	3.22
Su	3.33	3.33	3.33	0	0	90

(MMC)

Table 7.4. Confusion metrics for Cohn-Kanade Database using wavelet analysis.

-	A	D	F	H	S	Su
A	96.66	0	0	0	0	3.33
D	0	96.55	0	3.44	0	0
F	0	3.12	93.75	0	0	3.12
H	0	0	0	96.77	0	3.22
S	0	6.45	3.22	0	87.09	3.22
Su	0	6.66	10	3.33	0	80

(SVM)

-	A	D	F	H	S	Su
A	83.33	10	3.33	3.33	0	0
D	3.44	82.75	6.89	3.44	0	3.44
F	3.12	3.12	84.37	0	0	9.37
H	0	0	0	87.09	12.90	0
S	6.45	3.22	6.45	9.67	74.19	0
Su	0	0	10	3.33	0	86.66

(KNN)

-	A	D	F	H	S	Su
A	100	0	0	0	0	0
D	3.44	86.20	3.44	6.89	0	0
F	0	0	90.62	0	3.12	6.25
H	0	0	3.22	96.77	0	0
S	0	0	3.226	0	96.77	0
Su	0	6.66	10	0	0	83.33

(MLP)

(Table 7.3) cont.....

-	A	D	F	H	S	Su
A	83.33	6.66	6.66	3.33	0	0
D	3.44	89.65	3.44	0	3.44	0
F	3.12	3.12	78.12	0	9.37	6.25
H	0	0	3.22	90.32	6.45	0
S	12.90	0	9.67	0	77.41	0
Su	3.33	0	10	10	3.33	73.33

(KSTAR)

-	A	D	F	H	S	Su
A	93.33	3.33	0	3.33	0	0
D	3.44	86.20	3.44	0	3.44	3.44
F	0	0	96.87	0	0	3.12
H	0	0	0	100	0	0
S	3.22	0	0	0	93.54	3.22
Su	3.33	3.33	3.33	0	0	90

(MMC)

Table 7.5. Accuracy comparison with other systems based on Cohn-Kanade database.

Systems	Year	Features	Accuracy
Shan *et al.* [12]	2005	LBP and template matching	79.1%
M. Yeasin *et al.* [13]	2006	PCA with HMM	90.9%
Shan *et al.* [14]	2009	Gabor filter with SVM	86.8%
Meng, Zibo, *et al.* [26]	2017	IACNN	95.37%
Ali, Kamran et. al. [27]	2019	DE-GAN	97.28%
Liu, Daizong, *et al.* [28]	2020	CNN-LSTM Pooling	99.54%
Gera, Darshan, *et al.* [29]	2021	SCAN	97.31%
This study	**2022**	**Wavelet feature with SVM**	**97.8%**

Table 7.6. Accuracy comparison with other systems based on JAFFE database.

Systems	Year	Features	Accuracy
Bashyal *et al.* [30]	2008	Gabor filter	90.2
Koutlas *et al.*[31]	2008	Gabor filter	92.3

(Table 7.6) cont.....

Cheng *et al.* [20]	2010	Gaussian process	93.4
Oliveira *et al.* [32]	2011	PCA with SVM	94.0
U. Mlakar *et al.* [33]	2015	HOG and SVM	87.82
S. L. Happy *et al.* [34]	2015	features of salient facial patches	91.79
A. T. Lopes *et al.* [35]	2017	CNN	88.73
B. Yang, *et al.* [36]	2018	Deep Neural Network	92.21
This study	**2021**	**Wavelet features with SVM**	**93.4%**

CONCLUSION

This study exploited wavelet and curvelet analysis for emotion recognition in a noisy environment. Wavelet coefficient-based features performed well, especially in the presence of Gaussian noise and illumination changes for facial expression recognition. Although we have deployed the five best algorithms, the SVM classifier yields the best results for emotion recognition. Overall, we conclude that curvelet coefficients are well able to predict emotions even in noisy environments. Future work will evaluate the wavelet and curvelet coefficients on multimodal datasets (with many subjects) and other emotion dimensions.

REFERENCES

[1] M. Pantic, and L.J.M. Rothkrantz, "Facial action recognition for facial expression analysis from static face images", *IEEE Trans. Syst. Man Cybern. B Cybern.*, vol. 34, no. 3, pp. 1449-1461, 2004. [http://dx.doi.org/10.1109/TSMCB.2004.825931] [PMID: 15484916]

[2] M. Pantic, and L.J.M. Rothkrantz, "Automatic analysis of facial expressions: the state of the art", *IEEE Trans. Pattern Anal. Mach. Intell.*, vol. 22, no. 12, 2000.

[3] B. Fasel, and J. Luettin, "Automatic facial expression analysis: a survey", *Pattern Recognit.*, vol. 36, no. 1, pp. 259-275, 2003. [http://dx.doi.org/10.1016/S0031-3203(02)00052-3]

[4] Y. Tian, T. Kanade, and J. Cohn, *Facial Expression Analysis', Handbook of Face Recognition.* Springer, 2005, pp. 1424-1445.

[5] C. Yu, Y. Hua, and K. Zhao, "The method of human facial expression recognition based on wavelet transformation reducing the dimension and improved fisher discrimination", *3rd International Conference on Intelligent Networks and Intelligent Systems (ICINIS),* 2010pp. 43-47 [http://dx.doi.org/10.1109/ICINIS.2010.98]

[6] R. Zhi, and Q. Ruan, "Robust facial expression recognition using selected wavelet moment invariants", *WRI Global Congress on Intelligent Systems, GCIS '09,* 2009pp. 508-512 [http://dx.doi.org/10.1109/GCIS.2009.217]

[7] G.K. Verma, and B.K. Singh, "Facial emotion recognition in curvelet domain", *Commun. Comput. Inf. Sci.*, vol. 157, pp. 554-559, 2011. b [http://dx.doi.org/10.1007/978-3-642-22786-8_70]

[8] M. Mansoorizadeh, and N. Moghaddam Charkari, "Multimodal information fusion application to human emotion recognition from face and speech", *Multimedia Tools Appl.*, vol. 49, no. 2, pp. 277-297, 2010.

[http://dx.doi.org/10.1007/s11042-009-0344-2]

[9] A. Saha, and Q.M. Jonathan, "Facial Expression Recognition using Curvelet based local binary patterns", *IEEE International Conference on Acoustics Speech and Signal Processing (ICASSP),* 2010pp. 2470-2473 [http://dx.doi.org/10.1109/ICASSP.2010.5494892]

[10] X. Wu, and J. Zhao, "Curvelet feature extraction for face recognition and facial expression recognition", *Sixth International Conference on Natural Computation (ICNC),* 2010pp. 1212-1216 [http://dx.doi.org/10.1109/ICNC.2010.5583642]

[11] C.C. Lee, and C.Y. Shih, "Facial expression recognition using contourlets and regularized discriminant analysis-based boosting algorithm", *International Computer Symposium (ICS),* 2010pp. 1-5 [http://dx.doi.org/10.1109/COMPSYM.2010.5685519]

[12] C. Shan, S. Gong, and P.W. McOwan, "Robust facial expression recognition using local binary patterns", *IEEE International Conference on Image Processing,* vol. 2, 2005p. 2005

[13] M. Yeasin, B. Bullot, and R. Sharma, "Recognition of facial expressions and measurement of levels of interest from video", *IEEE Trans. Multimed.,* vol. 8, no. 3, pp. 500-508, 2006. [http://dx.doi.org/10.1109/TMM.2006.870737]

[14] C. Shan, S. Gong, and P.W. McOwan, "Facial expression recognition based on Local Binary Patterns: A comprehensive study", *Image Vis. Comput.,* vol. 27, no. 6, pp. 803-816, 2009. [http://dx.doi.org/10.1016/j.imavis.2008.08.005]

[15] Emi. , "Noise, dynamic range and bit depth in digital slrs", Available from: http://theory.uchicago.edu/ejm/pix/20d/tests/noise/ 2015.

[16] P. Carbnetto, N. de Freitas, and K. Barnard, "A statistical model for general contextual object recognition", *The 8th European Conference on Computer Vision,* 2004pp. 350-362 [http://dx.doi.org/10.1007/978-3-540-24670-1_27]

[17] M. Tuceryan, and A.K. Jain, *Texture Analysis' Handbook of pattern recognition and computer vision*, 1993.

[18] J.S. Weszka, C.R. Dyer, and A. Rosenfeld, "A comparative study of texture measures of Terrain classification", *IEEE Trans. Syst. Man Cybern.,* vol. SMC-6, no. 4, pp. 269-285, 1976. [http://dx.doi.org/10.1109/TSMC.1976.5408777]

[19] M. Lyons, S. Akamatsu, M. Kamachi, and J. Gyoba, "Coding facial expressions with gabor wavelets", *In Automatic Face and Gesture Recognition, 1998. Proceedings. Third IEEE International Conference on. IEEE,* 1998pp. 200-205 [http://dx.doi.org/10.1109/AFGR.1998.670949]

[20] Fei Cheng, Jiangsheng Yu, and Huilin Xiong, "Facial expression recognition in JAFFE dataset based on Gaussian process classification", *IEEE Trans. Neural Netw.,* vol. 21, no. 10, pp. 1685-1690, 2010. [http://dx.doi.org/10.1109/TNN.2010.2064176] [PMID: 20729164]

[21] A.M. Oliveira, M.P. Teixeira, I.B. Fonseca, and M. Oliveira, "Joint model-parameter validation of self-estimates of valence and arousal", *Probing a differential-weighting model of affective intensity. Proc. 22nd Ann. Meeting Int'l Soc. for Psychophysics,* 2006pp. 245-250

[22] John Platt, "Probabilistic outputs for support vector machines and comparisons to regularized likelihood methods", *Advances in large margin classifiers,* vol. 10.3, pp. 61-74, 1999.

[23] D.W. Aha, D. Kibler, and M.K. Albert, "Instance-based learning algorithms", *Mach. Learn.,* vol. 6, no. 1, pp. 37-66, 1991. [http://dx.doi.org/10.1007/BF00153759]

[24] J.G. Cleary, and L.E. Trigg, "K*: An Instance-based Learner Using an Entropic Distance Measure", *12th International Conference on Machine Learning,* 1995pp. 108-114 [http://dx.doi.org/10.1016/B978-1-55860-377-6.50022-0]

[25] N. Farajzadeh, G. Pan, Z. Wu, and M. Yao, "Multiclass classification based on meta probability codes", *Int. J. Pattern Recognit. Artif. Intell.*, vol. 25, no. 8, pp. 1219-1241, 2011. [http://dx.doi.org/10.1142/S021800141100910X]

[26] Z. Meng, "Identity-aware convolutional neural network for facial expression recognition", *2017 12th IEEE International Conference on Automatic Face & Gesture Recognition (FG 2017).*, 2017 [http://dx.doi.org/10.1109/FG.2017.140]

[27] K. Ali, and C.E. Hughes, "Facial expression recognition using disentangled adversarial learning", *arXiv*, 2019.

[28] D. Liu, X. Ouyang, S. Xu, P. Zhou, K. He, and S. Wen, "SAANet: Siamese action-units attention network for improving dynamic facial expression recognition", *Neurocomputing*, vol. 413, pp. 145-157, 2020. [http://dx.doi.org/10.1016/j.neucom.2020.06.062]

[29] D. Gera, and S. Balasubramanian, "Landmark guidance independent spatio-channel attention and complementary context information based facial expression recognition", *Pattern Recognit. Lett.*, vol. 145, pp. 58-66, 2021. [http://dx.doi.org/10.1016/j.patrec.2021.01.029]

[30] S. Bashyal, and G.K. Venayagamoorthy, "Recognition of facial expressions using Gabor wavelets and learning vector quantization", *Eng. Appl. Artif. Intell.*, vol. 21, no. 7, pp. 1056-1064, 2008. [http://dx.doi.org/10.1016/j.engappai.2007.11.010]

[31] A. Koutlas, and D.I. Fotiadis, "An automatic region based methodology for facial expression recognition", *IEEE International Conference on Systems, Man and Cybernetics*, 2008 [http://dx.doi.org/10.1109/ICSMC.2008.4811353]

[32] L. Oliveira, M. Mansano, A. Koerich, and A. de Souza Britto, "2d principal component analysis for face and facial-expression recognition", *Comput. Sci. Eng.*, vol. 13, no. 3, pp. 9-13, 2011. [http://dx.doi.org/10.1109/MCSE.2010.149]

[33] U. Mlakar, and B. Potočnik, "Automated facial expression recognition based on histograms of oriented gradient feature vector differences", *Signal Image Video Process.*, vol. 9, no. S1, pp. 245-253, 2015. [http://dx.doi.org/10.1007/s11760-015-0810-4]

[34] S.L. Happy, and A. Routray, "Automatic facial expression recognition using features of salient facial patches", *IEEE Trans. Affect. Comput.*, vol. 6, no. 1, pp. 1-12, 2015. [http://dx.doi.org/10.1109/TAFFC.2014.2386334]

[35] A.T. Lopes, E. de Aguiar, A.F. De Souza, and T. Oliveira-Santos, "Facial expression recognition with Convolutional Neural Networks: Coping with few data and the training sample order", *Pattern Recognit.*, vol. 61, pp. 610-628, 2017. [http://dx.doi.org/10.1016/j.patcog.2016.07.026]

[36] B. Yang, J. Cao, R. Ni, and Y. Zhang, "Facial expression recognition using weighted mixture deep neural network based on double-channel facial images", *IEEE Access*, vol. 6, pp. 4630-4640, 2018. [http://dx.doi.org/10.1109/ACCESS.2017.2784096]

CHAPTER 8

Spontaneous Emotion Recognition From Audio-Visual Signals

Abstract: This chapter introduces an emotion recognition system based on audio and video cues. For audio-based emotion recognition, we have explored various aspects of feature extraction and classification strategy and found that wavelet analysis is sound. We have shown comparative results for discriminating capabilities of various combinations of features using the Fisher Discriminant Analysis (FDA). Finally, we have combined the audio and video features using a feature-level fusion approach. All the experiments are performed with eNTERFACE and RML databases. Though we have applied multiple classifiers, SVM shows significantly improved performance with a single modality and fusion. The results obtained using fusion outperformed in contrast results based on a single modality of audio or video. We can conclude that fusion approaches are best as it is using complementary information from multiple modalities.

Keywords: Emotion recognition system, eNTERFACE, Feature fusion, Machine learning, RML database, Support vector machine.

8.1. INTRODUCTION

Most emotion recognition work is based on facial expression and vocal emotion [1, 2, 3, 4]. However, emotion modeling in a continuous space is completely lacking in the existing literature [5]; our book contributed in this direction by proposing an emotion model to predict a large number (more than fifteen) of complex emotions in a three-dimensional continuous space. Although we have implemented various systems to recognize emotion from speech, facial expression, physiological signals, and multimodal fusion of the above modalities, our emphasis is on emotion modeling in a continuous space.

This chapter investigates the use of audio-visual signals for spontaneous affect recognition. The proposed approach is based on Multiresolution analysis (MRA), which can analyze a signal at many resolutions. An MRA is the design process for the most practically important discrete wavelet transforms (DWT) and the reasoning for the Fast Wavelet Transform algorithm (FWT). MRA uses DWT to

Gyanendra K. Verma

extract the features. Different classifiers are used to classify the data, including the Support Vector Machine (SVM), Multilayer Perceptron (MLP), and K mean classifier. The MRA-based method in this book was created by building on prior work in emotion recognition using MRA [6]. Emotion recognition using audio and visual modalities is covered in this chapter.

The following is a breakdown of the chapter's structure. We review the many techniques for emotion recognition that have been reported in the literature. Then, using a development set of eNTERFACE [7] and RML [8] multimodal emotion databases, we present an emotion detection system based on auditory and visual cues and some of its main components. The use of multimodal fusion for emotion recognition is then investigated. Finally, experimental findings for audio and visual cues, as well as their combination utilizing feature level fusion, are shown on the eNTERFACE and RML databases.

8.2. RECOGNITION OF SPONTANEOUS EFFECTS

Affect recognition has been an emerging study subject within Human-Computer Interaction (HCI). Several affective states, including thinking, shame, and despair, are considered complex affective states and communicated *via* hundreds of distinct facial expressions. Researchers employed multimodal cues to identify emotion as a single cue may not correctly describe complex emotional states [9]. Several methods have been reported in the literature to extract characteristics from audio and visual cues.

8.3. THE DATABASE

Many academicians have been inspired to construct an emotion database due to recent breakthroughs in emotion identification.

- MIT [10],
- MMI [11],
- HUMAINE [12],
- VAM [13],
- SEMAINE [14],
- MAHNOB-HCI [15], and
- DEAP [16].

We used the eNTERFACE and RML audio-visual databases in this study. Fig. (**8.1**) depicts the facial expressions of various emotions for the eNTERFACE and RML databases. At the same time, Table **8.1** summarizes the database content for both databases.

8.3.1. eNTERFACE Database

The eNTERFACE05 is an audio and video emotion database that serves as a benchmark. Happy, Angry, Disgust, Sadness, Surprise, and Fear are the six primary emotions in the database. Forty-two people were involved in the collection of speech samples.

Fig. (8.1). Facial expressions for different emotions first row - eNTERFACE database, second row- RML database.

Table 8.1. Database content summary of eNTERFACE and RML database.

eNTERFACE	
Database type	Audiovisual
No. of subjects	44
Language	English
# Emotion	6 Universal emotions
#Video	1320
Image frame size	720*576
Frame rate	25
Audio sampling rate	48000
RML	
Database type	Audiovisual
No. of subjects	8
Language	6 (English, Mandarin, Urdu, Punjabi, Persian, Italian)

(Table 8.1) cont.....

eNTERFACE	
# Emotion	6 Universal emotions
#Video	720
Image frame size	720*480
Frame rate	30
Audio sampling rate	22050

8.3.2. RML Database

The RML emotion database, also an audio-visual emotion database, contains six basic universal emotions. The data samples were collected from movies taken from eight distinct themes and filmed in eight languages. While reading emotional lines, each participant was instructed to act naturally.

8.4. AUDIO-BASED EMOTION RECOGNITION SYSTEM

The acoustic properties of the audio stream are used to recognize emotions from auditory cues. There are numerous ways to capture acoustic properties, such as Mel Frequency Cepstral Coefficient (MFCC), Linear Predictive Coding (LPC), *etc.* MFCC, a cutting-edge method, is employed in this chapter for audio feature extraction. Diverse speech aspects, such as mood, speaker audio, and both, represent different speech information. As a result, experts are interested in learning more about the speech characteristics of various emotions. Vocal tract, prosodic, and excitation source characteristics are the three types of speech features [17].

Short segments of voice signals are used to extract Vocal Tract characteristics. These properties represent the energy distribution for a variety of speech frequencies. Various studies employ various vocal tract elements and their combinations for emotion identification. T. Long [18] employed the log frequency power coefficient (LFPC) vocal tract feature in conjunction with Perceptual Linear Prediction (PLP), MFCC, and LPCC to distinguish emotions, including Angry, Happy, Sad, Bored, and Neutral. They tested their system on a Mandarin database and found that it had an 84.2 percent recognition rate. Burmese-Mandarin corpus's database also assessed Linear prediction cepstral coefficients (LPCC) and MFCC features to recognize six universal emotions. The classification rates are reported at 56.1 percent and 59 percent for LPCC and MFCC, respectively.

The SAVEE database [19], employed Sub-band based Cepstral Parameter (SBC) and MFCC to recognize six emotions: Angry, Fear, Happy, Sad, Disgust, and Neutral, with a recognition rate of 79 percent [20]. The IITKGP-SEHSC [21] databases used to assess the effectiveness of MFCC in speaker-dependent and speaker-independent environments, using seven emotion categories: Angry, Disgust, Fear, Happy, Neutral, Sarcastic, and Surprise [20]. They discovered an 89.20 percent identification rate for speaker-dependent cases and a 48.18 percent recognition rate for speaker-independent cases.

As pitch has higher discriminating power than other prosodic variables, it is the most extensively employed prosodic feature for emotion identification. Aside from pitch log energy, one of the most important parameters for examining speaking styles and emotions is log energy [22]. They discovered that furious emotion could be separated from Fast, Lombard, Question, Slow, and Soft emotions using the log-energy feature of the SUSAS database [23]. Another important prosodic feature is the zero-crossing rates. The angry emotion has a higher mean value than the happy emotion due to the higher vibration frequency in speech signals.

Formants are another property that may be used to describe emotions in speech signals [24]. The formants feature is also used [25]. They found that furious had the most considerable formant frequency value compared to pleasure and sad, with sad having the lowest value. Few researchers [26, 27] have worked on excitation source information characteristics for creating emotion detection systems, which we have not evaluated in this research. We employed prosodic and spectral features of an audio signal to extract features.

8.4.1. Experiments

Experiments were carried out in two emotion databases, *i.e.*, eNTERFACE and RML database.

8.4.2. System Development

8.4.2.1. Audio Features

The initial configurations for the experiments are as follows:

MFCC : 12

Level of decomposition : 5

Coefficients : detail coefficient at each level and approximation at 5th level

Feature vector dimension : 32

The results for audio modality are shown in Tables **8.2** & **8.3**, and the confusion matrices for audio cues are shown in Tables **8.4** and **8.5**.

Table 8.2. Accuracy of AUDIO cue on eNTERFACE and RML database (A-Anger, D-Disgust, F-Fear, H-Happiness, S-Sadness, Sp-Surprise).

	-	A	D	F	H	S	Sp
eNTERFACE DATABASE	MLP	62.5	20.0	40.0	62.5	60.0	67.5
	SVM	60.0	37.5	35.0	72.5	45.0	40.0
RML DATABASE	MLP	74.17	62.50	46.67	55.83	70.83	68.33
	SVM	67.50	65.83	40	57.50	77.50	68.33

Table 8.3. Performance of AUDIO cue on eNTERFACE and RML database (A-Anger, D-Disgust, F-Fear, H-Happiness, S-Sadness, Sp-Surprise).

-		SVM			MLP		
-		Precision	Recall	F-measure	Precision	Recall	F-measure
eNTERFACE database	A	0.49	0.6	0.539	0.625	0.625	0.625
	D	0.357	0.375	0.366	0.348	0.2	0.254
	F	0.318	0.35	0.333	0.5	0.4	0.44
	H	0.644	0.725	0.682	0.595	0.625	0.61
	S	0.545	0.45	0.493	0.444	0.6	0.511
	Sp	0.593	0.4	0.478	0.551	0.675	0.607
RML Database	A	0.681	0.675	0.678	0.712	0.742	0.727
	D	0.594	0.658	0.625	0.591	0.625	0.607
	F	0.485	0.4	0.438	0.505	0.467	0.485
	H	0.556	0.575	0.566	0.545	0.558	0.551
	S	0.699	0.775	0.735	0.726	0.708	0.717
	Sp	0.732	0.683	0.707	0.701	0.683	0.692

Table 8.4. Confusion metrics for AUDIO cue based on RML Database(A-Anger, D-Disgust, F-Fear, H-Happiness, S-Sadness, Sp-Surprise).

-	A	D	F	H	S	Sp
A	**74.17**	3.33	0.83	6.67	0.00	15.00
D	1.67	**62.50**	15.00	15.83	4.17	0.83
F	9.17	16.67	**46.67**	7.50	12.50	7.50
H	5.00	16.67	6.67	**55.83**	10.00	5.83

(Table 8.4) cont.....

S	0.83	5.83	12.50	10.00	**70.83**	0.00
Sp	13.33	0.83	10.83	6.67	0.00	**68.33**

(MLP)

-	A	D	F	H	S	Sp
A	**67.50**	3.33	5.00	5.83	0.00	18.33
D	0.83	**65.83**	10.83	15.00	6.67	0.83
F	9.17	18.33	**40.00**	9.17	20.83	2.50
H	5.83	17.50	10.83	**57.50**	5.00	3.33
S	0.00	5.00	9.17	8.33	**77.50**	0.00
Sp	15.83	0.83	6.67	7.50	0.83	**68.33**

(SVM)

Table 8.5. Confusion metrics for AUDIO cue based on eNTERFACE Database (A-Anger, D-Disgust, F-Fear, H-Happiness, S-Sadness, Sp-Surprise).

-	A	D	F	H	S	Sp
A	**97.5**	0	0	0	1.25	1.25
D	2.5	**77.5**	8.75	3.75	5	2.5
F	1.25	1.25	**91.25**	0	3.75	2.5
H	0	1.25	1.25	**95**	1.25	1.25
S	2.5	2.5	0	2.5	**88.75**	3.75
Sp	3.75	1.25	1.25	2.5	10	**81.25**

(MLP)

-	A	D	F	H	S	Sp
A	**95**	0	0	0	5	0
D	0	**97.5**	0	0	0	2.5
F	0	7.75	**92.5**	0	0	0
H	0	0	0	**100**	0	0
S	0	2.5	0	0	**97.5**	0
Sp	2.5	6.25	2.5	0	0	**88.75**

(SVM)

8.5. VISUAL CUE-BASED EMOTION RECOGNITION SYSTEM

The following elements make up a face: The lips, nose, eyes, brows, chin, and cheeks all play a role in determining facial emotions and look. Single or mixtures of these face components can define facial expression. Ekman labeled the muscular activity of the upper facial components as "action units" (AUs). Geometric aspects in facial expressions were employed in several techniques. The most widely used algorithms for facial emotion identification are based on Ekman and Friesen's facial action coding system (FACS). Essa and Pentland [27] employed modular Eigen space for face localization.

Omid *et al.* proposed that facial image fields be oriented in a confined region while using a neural network to analyze facial emotions. We have opted for Spatio-temporal characteristics to detect small changes in a face. A geometric feature-based face analysis is challenging when changes occur due to lighting and position variations. We employ Dollar's approach to finding exciting regions within the images [28]. Munaf *et al.* [29] used an interactive evolutionary algorithm to investigate Dollar characteristics for human action retrievals. The Dollar's approach has been applied with audio elements for the human emotion identification system. We first apply linear separable filters to both sequences' spatial and temporal domains to obtain the response function.

8.5.1. Experiments

Experiments have been carried out in two emotion databases, *i.e.*, eNTERFACE and RML database.

8.5.2. System Development

8.5.2.1. Visual Feature

The initial configurations for the experiments are as follows:

Function : DB4

Level of decomposition : 5

Coefficients : detail coefficient at each level and approximation at 5th level

Feature vector dimension : 32

The results for visual modality are shown in Table **8.6** and **8.7**, and confusion metrics are shown in Tables **8.8** and **8.9**.

Table 8.6. VIDEO cue results for eNTERFACE and RML database (A-Anger, D-Disgust, F-Fear, H-Happiness, S-Sadness, Sp-Surprise).

-		SVM			MLP		
-		Precision	Recall	F-measure	Precision	Recall	F-measure
eNTERFACE database	A	0.495	0.588	0.537	0.826	0.713	0.765
	D	0.564	0.663	0.609	0.774	0.813	0.793
	F	0.533	0.6	0.565	0.75	0.75	0.75
	H	0.73	0.675	0.701	0.788	0.838	0.812
	S	0.606	0.538	0.57	0.78	0.8	0.79
	Sp	0.536	0.375	0.441	0.75	0.75	0.75
RML database	A	0.531	0.65	0.584	0.793	0.8	0.797
	D	0.621	0.683	0.651	0.785	0.792	0.788
	F	0.657	0.592	0.623	0.819	0.792	0.805
	H	0.678	0.667	0.672	0.805	0.825	0.815
	S	0.653	0.55	0.597	0.769	0.75	0.759
	Sp	0.719	0.683	0.701	0.828	0.842	0.835

Table 8.7. VIDEO cue results for eNTERFACE and RML database (A-Anger, D-Disgust, F-Fear, H-Happiness, S-Sadness, Sp-Surprise).

	-	A	D	F	H	S	Sp
eNTERFACE DATABASE	MLP	0.756	0.819	0.825	0.85	0.838	0.75
	SVM	0.625	0.744	0.631	0.706	0.694	0.65
RML DATABASE	MLP	0.8	0.792	0.792	0.825	0.75	0.842
	SVM	0.65	0.683	0.592	0.667	0.55	0.683

Table 8.8. Confusion metrics for Video based on RML Database (A-Anger, D-Disgust, F-Fear, H-Happiness, S-Sadness, Sp-Surprise).

-	A	D	F	H	S	Sp
A	**80.00**	2.50	2.50	5.00	1.67	8.33
D	4.17	**79.17**	7.50	4.17	4.17	0.83
F	5.00	5.83	**79.17**	0.00	5.83	4.17
H	5.00	6.67	1.67	**82.50**	3.33	0.83
S	3.33	5.00	3.33	10.00	**75.00**	3.33
Sp	3.33	1.67	2.50	0.83	7.50	**84.17**

(MLP)

(Table 8.8) cont.....

-	A	D	F	H	S	Sp
A	**65.00**	7.50	10.00	7.50	4.17	5.83
D	13.33	**68.33**	5.83	4.17	5.00	3.33
F	14.17	11.67	**59.17**	4.17	3.33	7.50
H	10.00	6.67	4.17	**66.67**	9.17	3.33
S	10.83	10.83	3.33	13.33	**55.00**	6.67
Sp	9.17	5.00	7.50	2.50	7.50	**68.33**

(SVM)

Table 8.9. Confusion metrics for Video based on RML Database (A-Anger, D-Disgust, F-Fear, H-Happiness, S-Sadness, Sp-Surprise).

-	A	D	F	H	S	Sp
A	**74.375**	7.5	7.5	4.375	3.125	3.125
D	3.75	**88.75**	3.125	1.25	1.25	1.875
F	4.375	5.625	**80**	0.625	4.375	5
H	3.75	1.875	1.125	**88.75**	0	4.375
S	3.125	1.125	5	1.125	**86.25**	3.125
Sp	5.625	3.75	3.75	3.75	3.75	**79.375**

(MLP)

-	A	D	F	H	S	Sp
A	**63.75**	4.375	8.75	6.875	7.5	8.75
D	15.625	**68.75**	4.375	5.625	3.75	1.875
F	13.75	5.625	**61.25**	1.875	8.125	9.375
H	11.25	11.875	1.25	**70.00**	0.625	5.00
S	10.00	4.375	13.1258	1.125	**69.375**	3.125
Sp	12.5	3.750	3.750	3.750	3.750	**62.50**

(SVM)

8.6. EXPERIMENTS BASED ON THE PROPOSED AUDIO-VISUAL CUES FUSION FRAMEWORK

This study makes use of both audio and visual signals for emotion recognition. The trials were carried out on both the RML and the eNTERFACE databases. A total of 1440 audio and video samples were utilised in the RML database. Similarly, 2640 audio and video samples were utilized to predict emotion in the eNTERFACE database. The audio and visual features are merged and sent into a feature selection method to determine the most discriminating features.

Table 8.10. Results based on single and combined cues for A) eNTERFACE and B) RML database (A-Anger, D-Disgust, F-Fear, H-Happiness, S-Sadness, Sp-Surprise).

-			SVM			MLP		
-			**Precision**	**Recall**	**F-measure**	**Precision**	**Recall**	**F-measure**
	Audio	**A**	0.974	0.95	0.962	0.907	0.975	0.94
		D	0.857	0.975	0.912	0.925	0.775	0.844
		F	0.974	0.925	0.949	0.89	0.913	0.901
		H	1	1	1	0.916	0.95	0.933
		S	0.951	0.975	0.963	0.807	0.888	0.845
		Sp	0.973	0.888	0.928	0.878	0.813	0.844
	-	**A**	0.495	0.588	0.537	0.826	0.713	0.765
	-	**D**	0.564	0.663	0.609	0.774	0.813	0.793
A) E N T E R F A C E D A T A B A S E	**Video**	**F**	0.533	0.6	0.565	0.75	0.75	0.75
	-	**H**	0.73	0.675	0.701	0.788	0.838	0.812
	-	**S**	0.606	0.538	0.57	0.78	0.8	0.79
	-	**Sp**	0.536	0.375	0.441	0.75	0.75	0.75
	Fusion	**A**	0.786	0.528	0.805	0.89	0.913	0.901
		D	0.71	0.825	0.763	0.87	0.838	0.854
		F	0.818	0.9	0.857	0.9	0.9	0.9
		H	0.823	0.813	0.818	0.89	0.913	0.901
		S	0.836	0.763	0.797	0.869	0913	0.89
		Sp	0.873	0.688	0.769	0.88	0.825	0.852

(Table 8.10) cont.....

-			SVM			MLP		
-			Precision	Recall	F-measure	Precision	Recall	F-measure
B) R M L D A T A B A S E	Audio	A	0.681	0.675	0.678	0.712	0.742	0.727
		D	0.594	0.658	0.625	0.591	0.625	0.607
		F	0.485	0.4	0.438	0.505	0.467	0.485
		H	0.556	0.575	0.566	0.545	0.558	0.551
		S	0.699	0.775	0.735	0.726	0.708	0.717
		Sp	0.732	0.683	0.707	0.701	0.683	0.692
	Video	A	0.531	0.65	0.584	0.793	0.8	0.797
		D	0.621	0.683	0.651	0.785	0.792	0.788
		F	0.657	0.592	0.623	0.819	0.792	0.805
		H	0.678	0.667	0.672	0.805	0.825	0.815
		S	0.653	0.55	0.597	0.769	0.75	0.759
		Sp	0.719	0.683	0.701	0.828	0.842	0.835
	Fusion	A	0.789	0.808	0.798	0.798	0.792	0.795
		D	0.721	0.817	0.766	0.807	0.8	0.803
		F	0.695	0.683	0.689	0.715	0.733	0.724
		H	0.795	0.742	0.767	0.791	0.758	0.774
		S	0.839	0.825	0.832	0.851	0.858	0.855
		Sp	0.858	0.808	0.943	0.813	0.833	0.823

Table 8.11. Multiple cue results for eNTERFACE and RML database (A-Anger, D-Disgust, F-Fear, H-Happiness, S-Sadness, Sp-Surprise).

	-	-	A	D	F	H	S	Sp
eNTERFACE DATABASE	MLP	Audio	62.5	20.0	40.0	62.5	60.0	67.5
		Video	75.6	81.9	82.5	85.0	83.8	75.0
		Fusion	**91.25**	**83.75**	**90**	**91.25**	**91.25**	**82.5**
	SVM	Audio	60.0	37.5	35.0	72.5	45.0	40.0
		Video	62.5	74.4	63.1	70.6	69.4	65.0
		Fusion	**79.17**	**80.0**	**73.33**	**75.83**	**85.83**	**83.33**

(Table 8.11) cont.....

RML DATABASE	**MLP**	Audio	74.17	62.50	46.67	55.83	70.83	68.33
		Video	80.0	79.17	79.17	82.50	75.0	84.17
		Fusion	**79.17**	**80.0**	**73.33**	**75.83**	**85.83**	**83.33**
	SVM	Audio	67.50	65.83	40.0	57.50	77.50	68.33
		Video	65.0	68.33	59.17	66.67	55.0	68.33
		Fusion	**80.83**	**81.67**	**68.33**	**74.17**	**82.50**	**80.83**

8.6.1. Results

The performance results for audio, video, and fusion (feature level) of audio-video cues using MLP and SVM classifier for eNTERFACE and RML databases are presented in Tables **8.10-8.13**. The results of the MLP and SVM classifiers are shown in Fig. (**8.2**). The visual cue system exceeds the auditory cue system. The combined system performed well compared to a single audio/video cue-based system.

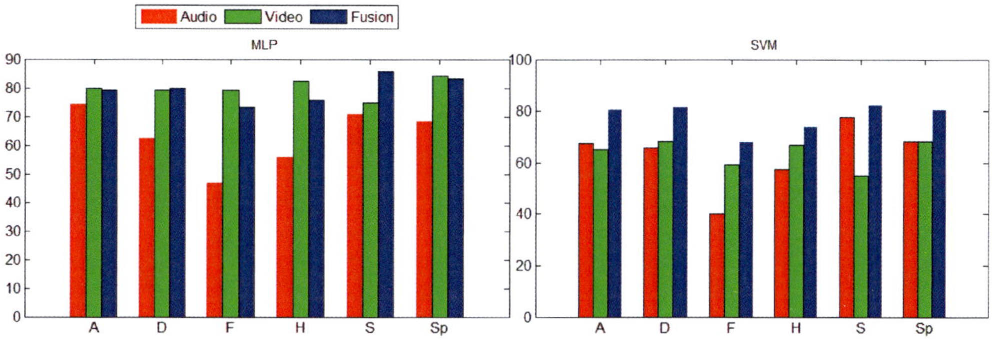

Fig. (8.2). Multiple cue results for RML database (A-Anger, D-Disgust, F-Fear, H-Happiness, S-Sadness, Sp-Surprise).

Table 8.12. Confusion metrics for Fusion of audio-video based on RML Database (A-Anger, D-Disgust, F-Fear, H-Happiness, S-Sadness, Sp-Surprise).

-	A	D	F	H	S	Sp
A	**79.17**	1.67	2.50	4.17	0.00	12.50
D	1.67	**80.00**	10.00	5.83	2.50	0.00
F	5.00	9.17	**73.33**	1.67	7.50	3.33
H	5.00	6.67	5.00	**75.83**	4.17	3.33
S	0.83	1.67	5.83	5.83	**85.83**	0.00
Sp	7.50	0.00	5.83	2.50	0.83	**83.33**

(MLP)

(Table 8.12) cont.....

-	A	D	F	H	S	Sp
A	**80.83**	1.67	3.33	5.00	0.00	9.17
D	1.67	**81.67**	9.17	4.17	3.33	0.00
F	4.17	15.00	**68.33**	3.33	7.50	1.67
H	4.17	10.00	4.17	**74.17**	5.00	2.50
S	0.00	4.17	7.50	5.83	**82.50**	0.00
Sp	11.67	0.83	5.83	0.83	0.00	**80.83**

(SVM)

Table 8.13. Confusion metrics for Fusion of audio-video based on eNTERFACE Database (A-Anger, D-Disgust, F-Fear, H-Happiness, S-Sadness, Sp-Surprise).

-	A	D	F	H	S	Sp
A	**91.25**	2.5	1.25	2.5	1.25	1.25
D	3.75	**83.75**	2.5	2.5	2.5	5
F	1.25	2.5	**90**	0	3.75	2.5
H	2.5	3.75	0	**91.25**	1.25	1.25
S	0	0	3.75	3.75	**91.25**	1.25
Sp	3.75	3.75	2.5	2.5	5	**82.5**

(MLP)

-	A	D	F	H	S	Sp
A	**82.5**	5	2.5	6.25	2.5	1.25
D	5	**82.5**	2.5	3.75	3.75	2.5
F	1.25	3.75	**90**	0	2.5	2.5
H	6.25	6.25	1.25	**81.25**	3.75	1.25
S	3.75	8.75	5	3.75	**76.25**	2.5
Sp	6.25	10	8.75	3.75	2.5	**68.75**

(SVM)

8.6.2. Comparison To Other Research

Table **8.14** compares the accuracy of different systems based on audio-visual emotion recognition. Our system's average accuracy (based on MLP) is 88.3 percent, which is much higher than the performance of other systems, as shown in Table **8.14**.

Table 8.14. Accuracy comparison with other systems based on Audio-Visual Emotion Recognition.

Systems	Year	Features	Accuracy (%)
Schuller B. *et al.* [30]	2009	Arousal- valance	80.2 for SVM & 80.5 for HMM/GMM
Datcu D. *et al.* [31]	2009	Facial features	85 through SVM
Mansoorizadeh M. *et al.* [32]	2010	Asynchronous Feature level fusion	84
Paleari M. *et al.* [33]	2010	Neural network	71
Wang Y. *et al.* [34]	2012	kernel cross-modal factor analysis	72.4
Tzirakis, Panagiotis, *et al.*[35]	2017	CNN, Resnet LSTM Feature-level	78.80
Nguyen, Dung, *et al.*[36]	2017	C3D + DBN Score-level	89.39
Chen, Junkai, *et al.*[37]	2018	Acoustic, Geometric and HOG-TOP Multiple kernel	88.2
Hossain, M. Shamim *et al.*[38]	2019	2D CNN, 3D CNN ELM-based	78.42
Zhao, Sicheng, *et al.*[39]	2020	2D/ 3D ResNet + Attention	54.50
Hao, Man, *et al.*[40]	2020	Multitask CNN Meta-Classifier	81.36
Our study	2022	wavelet analysis	88.3

CONCLUSION

This chapter introduced an emotion identification system based on audio and visual inputs. This study extensively analyzed audio-visual signals using different machine learning approaches and with the five best classifiers for spontaneous emotion recognition. The feature-level fusion of audio-visual signals is applied to classify spontaneous emotions. The findings produced utilizing fusions outperform the single-mode cues-based system.

REFERENCES

[1] Y.V. Venkatesh, A.A. Kassim, J. Yuan, and T.D. Nguyen, "On the simultaneous recognition of identity and expression from BU-3DFE datasets", *Pattern Recognit. Lett.,* vol. 33, no. 13, pp. 1785-1793, 2012.
[http://dx.doi.org/10.1016/j.patrec.2012.05.015]

[2] M. El Ayadi, M.S. Kamel, and F. Karray, "Survey on speech emotion recognition: Features, classification schemes, and databases", *Pattern Recognit.,* vol. 44, no. 3, pp. 572-587, 2011.
[http://dx.doi.org/10.1016/j.patcog.2010.09.020]

[3] Y. Rahulamathavan, R.C.W. Phan, J.A. Chambers, and D.J. Parish, "Facial expression recognition in

the encrypted domain based on local fisher discriminant analysis", *IEEE Trans. Affect. Comput.,* vol. 4, no. 1, pp. 83-92, 2013.
[http://dx.doi.org/10.1109/T-AFFC.2012.33]

[4] Y.H. Yang, Y.C. Lin, Y.F. Su, and H.H. Chen, "A regression approach to music emotion recognition", *IEEE Trans. Audio Speech Lang. Process.,* vol. 16, no. 2, pp. 448-457, 2008.
[http://dx.doi.org/10.1109/TASL.2007.911513]

[5] J. Broekens, C.M. Jonker, and J.J.C. Meyer, "Affective negotiation support systems", *J. Ambient Intell. Smart Environ.,* vol. 2, no. 2, pp. 121-144, 2010.
[http://dx.doi.org/10.3233/AIS-2010-0065]

[6] G.K. Verma, U.S. Tiwary, and M.K. Rai, "Facial emotion recognition using different multi-resolution transforms", *Commun. Comput. Inf. Sci.,* vol. 192, pp. 469-477, 2011.
[http://dx.doi.org/10.1007/978-3-642-22720-2_49]

[7] O. Martin, I. Kotsia, B. Macq, and I. Pitas, "The eNTERFACE 05 Audio-Visual Emotion Database", *Proc. of the First IEEE Workshop on Multimedia Database Management,* 2006 Atlanta

[8] Y. Wang, and L. Guan, "Recognizing human emotional state from audiovisual signals", *IEEE Trans. Multimed.,* vol. 10, no. 4, pp. 659-668, 2008.
[http://dx.doi.org/10.1109/TMM.2008.921734]

[9] H. Gunes, B. Schuller, M. Pantic, and R. Cowie, "Emotion representation, analysis and synthesis in continuous space: A survey",
[http://dx.doi.org/10.1109/FG.2011.5771357]

[10] J.A. Healey, and R.W. Picard, "Detecting stress during real-world driving tasks using physiological sensors", *IEEE Trans. Intell. Transp. Syst.,* vol. 6, no. 2, pp. 156-166, 2005.
[http://dx.doi.org/10.1109/TITS.2005.848368]

[11] M. Pantic, M. Valstar, R. Rademaker, and L. Maat, "Web-based database for facial expression analysis", *Proc. IEEE Int'l Conf. Multimedia and Expo,* 2005pp. 317-321

[12] E. Douglas-Cowie, R. Cowie, I. Sneddon, C. Cox, O. Lowry, M. McRorie, J.C. Martin, L. Devillers, S. Abrilian, A. Batliner, N. Amir, and K. Karpouzis, "The HUMAINE Database: Addressing the collection and annotation of naturalistic and induced emotional data", *Proc. Second Int'l Conf. Affective Computing and Intelligent Interaction,* 2007pp. 488-500
[http://dx.doi.org/10.1007/978-3-540-74889-2_43]

[13] M. Grimm, K. Kroschel, and S. Narayanan, "The Vera am Mittag German Audio-Visual Emotional Speech Database", *Proc. IEEE Int'l Conf. Multimedia and Expo,* 2008pp. 865-868
[http://dx.doi.org/10.1109/ICME.2008.4607572]

[14] G. McKeown, M.F. Valstar, R. Cowie, and M. Pantic, "The SEMAINE Corpus of Emotionally Colored Character Interactions", *Proc. IEEE Int'l Conf. Multimedia and Expo,* 2010pp. 1079-1084

[15] M. Soleymani, Jeroen Lichtenauer, Thierry Pun, and Maja Pantic, "A Multimodal Database for Affect Recognition and Implicit Tagging", In: *IEEE Tran. On Affective Computing* vol. 3. , 2012no. 1, .

[16] S. Koelstra, C. Muhl, M. Soleymani, Jong-Seok Lee, A. Yazdani, T. Ebrahimi, T. Pun, A. Nijholt, and I. Patras, "DEAP: A database for emotion analysis; using physiological signals", *IEEE Trans. Affect. Comput.,* vol. 3, no. 1, pp. 18-31, 2012.
[http://dx.doi.org/10.1109/T-AFFC.2011.15]

[17] Shien Shing Oij, "A new approach of audio emotion recognition", *J. of Expert Systems with Applications,* vol. 41, pp. 5858-5869, 2014.

[18] Z. Long, G. Liu, and X. Dai, "Extracting emotional features from ECG by using wavelet transform", *International Conference on Biomedical Engineering and Computer Science,* 2010pp. 1-4
[http://dx.doi.org/10.1109/ICBECS.2010.5462441]

[19] K.V. Kishore,

[20] M. Bhaykar, J. Yadav, and K. Sreenivasa Rao, "Speaker dependent, speaker independent and cross language emotion recognition from speech using GMM and HMM", 2013. [http://dx.doi.org/10.1109/NCC.2013.6487998]

[21] K. Sreenivasa Rao, Shashidhar G Koolagudi, and Ramu Reddy Vempada, "Emotion recognition from speech using global and local prosodic features", *International Journal of Speech Technology,* vol. 15, no. 3, pp. 1-18, 2012.

[22] M. Kammoun, and N. Ellouze, "Spectral features detection of speech emotion and speaking styles recognition based on HMM classifier", *5th WSEAS Int. conf. on Signal processing,* 2006pp. 1-5 USA

[23] JHL Hansen, and S Bou-Ghazale, "A novel training approach for improving speech recognition under adverse stressful environments", *EUROSPEECH-97,* 1997.

[24] M. Goudbeek, D. Swingley, and R. Smits, "Supervised and unsupervised learning of multidimensional acoustic categories", *J. Exp. Psychol. Hum. Percept. Perform.,* vol. 35, no. 6, pp. 1913-1933, 2009. [http://dx.doi.org/10.1037/a0015781] [PMID: 19968443]

[25] J. Přibil, A. Přibilová, and I. Frollo, "Analysis of spectral properties of acoustic noise produced during magnetic resonance imaging", *Appl. Acoust.,* vol. 73, no. 8, pp. 687-697, 2012. [http://dx.doi.org/10.1016/j.apacoust.2012.01.007]

[26] K.E. Cummings, and M.A. Clements, "Analysis of the glottal excitation of emotionally styled and stressed speech", *J. Acoust. Soc. Am.,* vol. 98, no. 1, pp. 88-98, 1995. [http://dx.doi.org/10.1121/1.413664] [PMID: 7608410]

[27] I.A. Essa, T. Darrell, and A. Pentland, "Tracking Facial Motion", *Proceedings of the IEEE Workshop on No rigid and Articulate Motion,* 1994pp. 36-42

[28] P. Dollar, V. Rabaud, G. Cottrell, and S. Belongie, "Behaviors recognition via sparse spatio-temporal features", *VS-PETS,* vol. 2005, pp. 65-72, 2005.

[29] S. Munaf, and F. Nasir, "Emotional Intelligence and Academics of Adolescents: A Correlational and Gender Comparative Study", *J. Behav. Sci.,* vol. 21, p. 2, 2011.

[30] B. Schuller, "Acoustic emotion recognition: A benchmark comparison of performances", *Proc. IEEE ASRU,* 2009 [http://dx.doi.org/10.1109/ASRU.2009.5372886]

[31] D. Datcu, and L.J. Rothkrantz, "The recognition of emotions from speech using gentleboost classifier: a comparison approach", *Proc. Int'l Conf. Computer Systems and Technologies,* vol. vol. 1, 2006pp. 1-6

[32] M. Mansoorizadeh, and N. Moghaddam Charkari, "Multimodal information fusion application to human emotion recognition from face and speech", *Multimedia Tools Appl.,* vol. 49, no. 2, pp. 277-297, 2010. [http://dx.doi.org/10.1007/s11042-009-0344-2]

[33] M. Paleari, R. Chellali, and B. Huet, "Features for multimodal emotion recognition: an extensive study", *Proc. CIS,* 2010pp. 90-95 [http://dx.doi.org/10.1109/ICCIS.2010.5518574]

[34] Y. Wang, L. Guan, and A. Venetsanopoulos, *Kernel cross-modal factor analysis for information fusion with application to bimodal emotion recognition*, 2012.

[35] P. Tzirakis, G. Trigeorgis, M.A. Nicolaou, B.W. Schuller, and S. Zafeiriou, "End-to-end multimodal emotion recognition using deep neural networks", *IEEE J. Sel. Top. Signal Process.,* vol. 11, no. 8, pp. 1301-1309, 2017. [http://dx.doi.org/10.1109/JSTSP.2017.2764438]

[36] D. Nguyen, *"Deep spatio-temporal features for multimodal emotion recognition." 2017 IEEE winter conference on applications of computer vision (WACV).* IEEE, 2017.

[37] J. Chen, Z. Chen, Z. Chi, and H. Fu, "Facial expression recognition in video with multiple feature fusion", *IEEE Trans. Affect. Comput.,* vol. 9, no. 1, pp. 38-50, 2018. [http://dx.doi.org/10.1109/TAFFC.2016.2593719]

[38] M.S. Hossain, and G. Muhammad, "Emotion recognition using deep learning approach from audio–visual emotional big data", *Inf. Fusion,* vol. 49, pp. 69-78, 2019. [http://dx.doi.org/10.1016/j.inffus.2018.09.008]

[39] S. Zhao, Y. Ma, Y. Gu, J. Yang, T. Xing, P. Xu, R. Hu, H. Chai, and K. Keutzer, "An end-to-end visual-audio attention network for emotion recognition in user-generated videos", *Proc. Conf. AAAI Artif. Intell.,* vol. 34, no. 1, pp. 303-311, 2020. [http://dx.doi.org/10.1609/aaai.v34i01.5364]

[40] Hao, and Man, "Visual-audio emotion recognition based on multi-task and ensemble learning with multiple features", *Neurocomputing,* vol. 391, pp. 42-51, 2020.

CHAPTER 9

Multimodal Fusion Framework: Emotion Recognition From Physiological Signals

Abstract: This study presents a multimodal fusion framework for emotion recognition from physiological signals. In contrast to emotion recognition through facial expression, a large number of emotions can be recognized accurately through physiological signals. The DEAP database, a benchmark multimodal database with many collections of EEG and peripheral signals, is employed for experimentation. The proposed method takes into account those features that are subject-independent and can incorporate many more emotions. As it is possible to handle many channel features, especially synchronous EEG channels, feature-level fusion is applied in this study. The features extracted from EEG and peripheral signals include relative, logarithmic, and absolute power energy of Alpha, Beta, Gamma, Delta, and Theta. Experimental results demonstrate that physiological signals' Theta and Beta bands are the most significant contributor to the performance. On the other hand, SVM performs outstandingly.

Keywords: 3D emotion model, EEG, Facial expression, Fusion framework, Physiological signal.

9.1. INTRODUCTION

Physiological cues are essential in determining whether or not a person's behavior or emotional state has changed. Physiological signals are biosignals such as Galvanic Skin Response (GSR), Respiration amplitude, Electrocardiogram (ECG), Electro-mayograms (EMG), Electrooculogram (EOG), Electro Dermal Activity (EDA), Galvanic Skin Response (GSR), Skin Conductance Response (SCR), and skin temperature [1]. EDA and GSR are skin conductance measurements extensively utilized for automated emotion identification. According to Kim J., GSR is a relatively reliable physiological marker of human arousal [2]. EEG, EMG, Skin conductance, BVP, and other physiological signals can be employed for emotion identification.

Electroencephalogram (EEG) is used in this study. EEG measures voltage changes in the brain's neurons induced by ionic current flows. For a brief length of time, 20–40 minutes, several electrodes put on the scalp capture the brain's spont-

Gyanendra K. Verma

aneous electrical activity. A brief introduction of various bio signals is given. A typical architecture of emotion recognition from physiological signals is illustrated in Fig. (**9.1**).

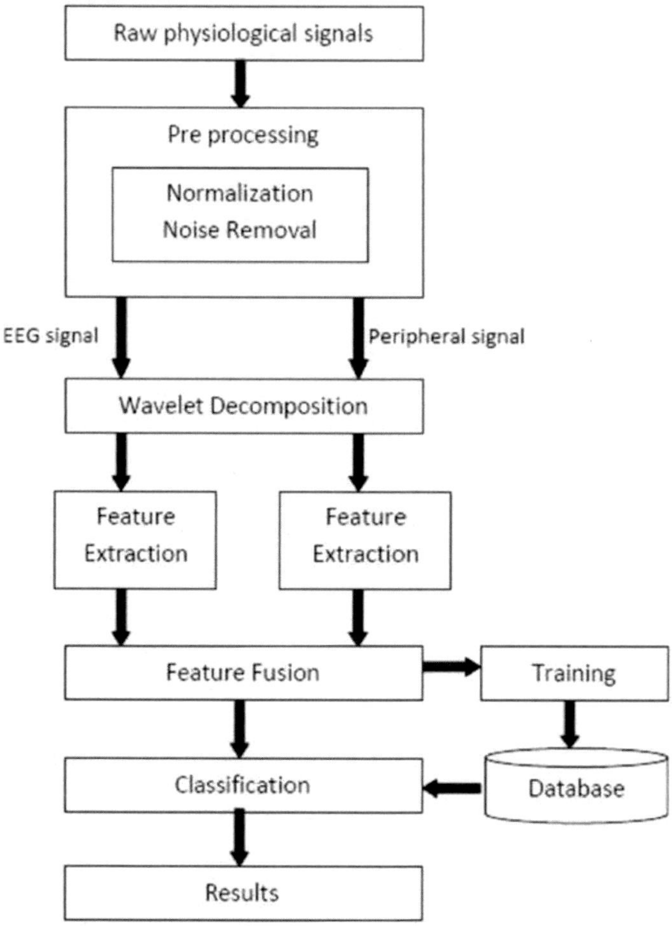

Fig. (9.1). Architecture of emotion recognition from physiological signal.

9.1.1. Electrical Brain Activity

EEG is a technique for detecting continuous electrical brain activity with amplitudes ranging from 1 to 200 microvolts. The 10-20 electrode placement approach is the most prevalent. Hundreds of electrodes (roughly) are implanted in the skull depending on its geometric dimensions.

9.1.2. Muscle Activity

Electromyography measures the electrical potentials that muscle fibers generate from muscular contraction (EMG). Ekman *et al.* [3] stated that facial EMG could give a sensitive and objective metric for emotion recognition as some facial muscles cannot be engaged voluntarily.

9.1.3. Skin Conductivity

The skin's electrical resistance is measured by skin conductance and regulated by the activity of the preparatory glands. The greater the skin conductance, the more active the preparation glands are.

9.1.4. Skin Temperature

According to McFarland [4], stimulating negative emotions causes skin temperature to drop, but calm, pleasant emotions cause skin temperature to rise. Emotion identification may also be made using heart rate and respiratory rate. Different physiological signals may be integrated to increase the accuracy of emotion identification.

Many Physiological signals are vital for emotion, according to several emotion theories. Ekman [5] proved that a particular physiological pattern might be linked to a specific emotion. For feature extraction, two types of data are employed in this study: EEG and peripheral. Frequency and amplitude are two parameters that may be used to define EEG. The EEG signal may be categorized into different bands based on frequency: Alpha, Beta, Gamma, Delta, and Theta. The frequency range of the above bands are 1 - 4 Hz., 4 - 8 Hz., 8 -12.5 Hz., 12.5 - 28 Hz. and 30-40 Hz, respectively.

9.2. MULTIMODAL EMOTION DATABASE

The availability of multimodal datasets is an essential factor in evaluating the performance of a pattern recognition system. The following are the multimodal databases that are currently available:

- HUMAINE database: This is an audiovisual database with gestures.
- Audiovisual database of Belfast naturalists.
- Smartkom combines audiovisual and gestural input.
- Salas audiovisual database.

- Oresteia database: audio and physiological information.
- XM2VTSDB: audiovisual multimodal face database.
- ISLE corpora: audiovisual + gestural.

Many academics have been inspired to construct an emotion database due to recent breakthroughs in emotion identification. MIT [6], MMI [7], HUMAINE [8], VAM [9], SEMAINE [10], MAHNOB-HCI [11], and DEAP [12]. This study makes use of the DEAP database. Speech, visual or audiovisual data, and physiological mood data are all stored in these databases.

9.2.1. DEAP Database

DEAP is a multimodal emotion that includes physiological inputs from 32 people as well as frontal face footage from 22 others. Each participant was instructed to keep track of their emotional responses regarding arousal, valence, dominance, likes, and familiarity while watching the movies [12]. Thirty-two subjects' electroencephalograms (EEGs) and peripheral physiological data were recorded at 512 Hz utilizing 32 electrodes.

Prior to categorization and emotion identification, raw data must be preprocessed. The preprocessing of the DEAP database was done using the following stages:

- The dataset is down-sampled to 128Hz as a preprocessing step.
- EOG artifacts were removed.
- Used a 4.0-45.0Hz bandpass frequency filter.
- Using a common reference point to average the data.

9.3. FEATURE EXTRACTION

Most emotion theory demonstrates that physiological characteristics are essential in emotion recognition. A physiological pattern is linked to a particular emotion, according to [5]. For feature extraction, two types of data were employed in this study: EEG and peripheral physiological signals. Frequency and amplitude are two parameters that may be used to define EEG. The EEG signal contains five frequency bands: Alpha, Beta, Gamma, Theta, and Delta [13]. Following attributes are considered as features to analyze the EEG data:

- Relative Power Energy (E_{RPE})
- Logarithmic Relative Power Energy (E_{LRPE})
- Absolute Logarithmic Relative Power Energy (E_{EALRPE})

The above features were recovered from EEG data for each frequency band (Delta, Theta, Alpha, Beta, and Gamma). For each degree of detail coefficients and maximum level of approximation coefficient, Standard deviation and Entropy were determined in addition to Power spectral characteristics. From physiological signals, a total of 25 characteristics were retrieved.

The sub-band energy can be calculated from Equation **1**

$$E_j = \sum_k (d_j(k))^2 \quad \textbf{(1)}$$

Where E_j is the subband energy in the jth frequency band.

E_{RPE}, E_{LRPE} and E_{ALRPE} can be calculated byequations **2**, **3** and **4**, respectively.

$$E_{RPE} = \frac{E_j}{E_{TOTAL}} \quad \textbf{(2)}$$

Where $E_{TOTAL} = E_{Alpha} + E_{Beta} + E_{Gamma} + E_{Theta}$

$$E_{LRPE} = \log(E_{RPE}) \quad \textbf{(3)}$$

$$E_{ALRPE} = \text{abs}(E_{LRPE}) \quad \textbf{(4)}$$

9.3.1. Feature Extraction from EEG

Wavelet analysis is used to extract characteristics from preprocessed EEG data. To calculate the approximation and detail coefficients, the EEG data is divided into four levels. Signal decomposition up to four levels is sufficient to capture useful information because the EEG signal is sampled at 512 Hz. Wavelet features are created using approximation and detail coefficients.

For wavelet analysis of EEG data, the Discrete Wavelet Transform (DWT) is used with the Daubechies 4 family (DB4). This work uses the Daubechies wavelet family, which delivers good results in quasi-signal processing [14].

9.3.2. Feature Extraction from Peripheral Signals

EDA and GSR are skin conductance measurements extensively utilized for automated emotion identification. GSR was found to be a reasonably reliable physiological marker of human arousal by J. Kim *et al.* [2]. The following features were extracted from EEG and physiological signals:

1. Relative Power Energy (RPE): Four bands of Delta, Theta, Alpha, Beta, and Gamma.

2. Logarithmic Relative Power Energy (LRPE): Four bands of Delta, Theta, Alpha, Beta, and Gamma.

3. Absolute Logarithmic Relative Energy: all four bands and Power energy (ALRPE) and Gamma.

4. Entropy and Standard deviation: detail coefficients at all levels and highest level approximation coefficient.

9.4. CLASSIFICATION AND RECOGNITION OF EMOTION

The initial stage in the pattern recognition task must be categorization. Several pattern recognition approaches have been documented in the literature on machine learning. To arrive at the final decision, we used Support Vector Machine (SVM) and K-Nearest Neighbor (KNN) classifiers in this study.

9.4.1. Support Vector Machine (SVM)

The most extensively used machine learning techniques for regression and classification issues are support vector machines (SVMs). Both linear and non-linear classification is possible with the SVM. Non-linear classification is achieved using the Kernel function. The kernels in non-linear classification are polynomial, radial basis function, and hyperbolic tangent function. SVM performs particularly well using the Gaussian kernel, which has only one parameter. The SVM strategy is the most widely used machine learning methodology, particularly in industrial settings, because it outperforms the others. The SVM methodology is commonly recognized as the most successful method for non-linear dataset categorization. The SVM technique has potential downsides when processing large volumes of data, such as increased memory utilization.

The solved SVM algorithm's parameters are tough to grasp. All input data must be accurately labeled before employing the SVM technique. The SVM method provides the advantage of improved classification accuracy and analysis performance.

The equation for the SVM can be given as:

$$g(x) = w^T x + b$$
$$g(x) \geq 1, \quad \forall x \in Class1 \qquad \textbf{(5)}$$
$$g(x) \leq 1, \quad \forall x \in Class2$$

Where w is a hyperplane vector, b is the bias, and g(x) is the classifier.

The following Equation **6** is used to compute the distance between two hyperplanes that are close to the support vector of two classes:

$$M = 2/(||w||) \qquad \textbf{(6)}$$

The basic purpose of maximising the margin is to minimise the value of ||w|| until no data points exist between the two hyperplanes. The main goal is to figure out w and b in such a way that:

$$\varphi(w) = {}^1/_2\, |w|^2 \; is\; maximized\; and\; subject\; to\; \forall(x_i y_i) : \; y_i(w^T x_i + b) \geq 1$$

The aforementioned issue is addressed using a quadratic equation, and the answer is as follows:

$$w = \sum_{i=1}^{n} \alpha_i y_i x_i \qquad \textbf{(7)}$$

Where α_i is the Lagrange multiplier. So the equation of SVM classifier is given as:

$$g(x) = \sum_{i=1}^{n} \alpha_i y_i x_i . X \qquad \textbf{(8)}$$

Non-linear SVM maps non-linear data into an HD feature space utilizing kernel functions, including polynomial, radial basis, and hyperbolic tangent. The multi-class SVM is used to sort training data into more than two groups.

9.4.2. Multi-Layer Perceptron (MLP)

A perceptron is the most straightforward neural network architecture. An MLP consists of multiple layers in contrast to a perceptron, with only one layer. MLP falls under supervised learning and utilizes Backpropagation to train the model.

A multilayer perceptron is distinguished by the fact that it uses a non-linear activation function to simulate the frequency of action potentials, or firing, of genuine neurons in the brain.

This function can be represented in a variety of ways. Both sigmoid activation functions are employed in contemporary applications and are defined by equation **10**:

$$y(v_i) = tanh(v_i) \; and \; y(v_i) = (1 + e^{-v_i})^{-1} \quad \textbf{(9)}$$

The first function in equation 3.10 is a hyperbolic tangent with a range of -1 to 1, whereas the second, the logistic function, has a similar shape but a range of 0 to 1. The weighted total of the input synapses is vi, while yi is the output of the ith node (neuron).

9.4.3. K-Nearest Neighbor (K-NN)

The K-Nearest Neighbor (K-NN) method is a non-parametric learning technique for classifying objects into multiple categories. As it does not use the training data for generalization, it is also known as the lazy algorithm. As a result of the above, the training phase is rapid, and the testing phase makes use of all of the training data. As a result, the testing step of the k-NN method is more time and space-intensive than the testing phase of other classification algorithms.

In the k-NN algorithm, k defines the number of nearest neighbors the model considers. With k = 1, the model is known as the closest neighbor. The distance measurement can be done using distance functions like Euclidean, Manhattan, Minkowski, or City-block distance.

Suppose there is an n-dimensional data point X = [$x_{1,}$ x_2....x_n], which is to be classified, then the *k*-NN algorithm finds a point that is closest to X and assigns the class label of that point to X. The distance between two data points is calculated by using Equation **11**.

$$dis(X_i, X_j) = |T(X_i, X_j)| \quad \textbf{(10)}$$

Where *T* (X_i, *Xj)* is any distance function specified above.

9.5. RESULTS AND DISCUSSION

This study has performed analysis and assessment as - 1) A categorical model of emotion is used to identify emotion from EEG and peripheral physiological signals, and 2) presentation of 3D emotion in VAD space. All of the experiments make use of the DEAP database. Experiments employed 40 channel EEG signals with 8056 data and 40 trials per subject for 32 people.

9.5.1. Emotion Categorization Results Based On The Proposed Multimodal Fusion Architecture

Multiresolution analysis was performed to extract attributes from thirty-two EEG and eight peripheral channel data of more than 8000 samples. To estimate the approximation and detail coefficients, the Wavelet Transform, a commonly used transform for multiresolution analysis, is utilized to decompose the signals. Signal decomposition up to five levels is adequate to retrieve significant attributes from physiological signals at a sampling rate of 512 Hz. The Discrete Wavelet Transform (DWT) using the Daubechies 4 family is used by [14] because it produces good results from EEG signals.

In this experiment, the features were extracted using multiresolution analysis of physiological data from 32 EEG channels and eight peripheral signals. The Wavelet Transform, a frequently used transform for multiresolution analysis, is used to split the signals up to five levels in order to determine the approximation and detail coefficients. The sample rate is 512 Hz, and signal decomposition up to five levels is sufficient to recover physiological signals, utilizing the Discrete Wavelet Transform (DWT) with the Daubechies 4 family because it delivers good results for non-stationary signals like EEG (DB4) [14].

For data categorization, the Waikato Environment for Knowledge Analysis [15] programme was utilised, which provides a suite of machine learning methods. Based on the maximum classification accuracy, we chose four approaches: Support Vector Machine (SVM), Multilayer Perceptron (MLP), K-Nearest Neighbor (K-NN), and Meta-multiclass (MMC). Fig. (**9.2**) shows the accuracies obtained with 32 EEG channel data and each classifier for each emotion.

SVM, MLP, KNN, and MMC had average accuracies of 81.45 percent, 74.37 percent, 57.74 percent, and 75.94 percent, respectively. “Depressing” had the best accuracy, with 85.46 percent using SVM. SVM outperformed in comparison to other classifiers, as shown in Fig. (**9.2**). A polynomial kernel was used to implement the SVM. The parameter d determines the order of the polynomial in the polynomial kernel. The regression curve becomes increasingly convoluted as d increases. The cost parameter C determines the impact of each support vector. We experimented with several C values (100, 200, 500, *etc.*) and discovered that C=200 produces the best results. As a result, we settled on C = 200.

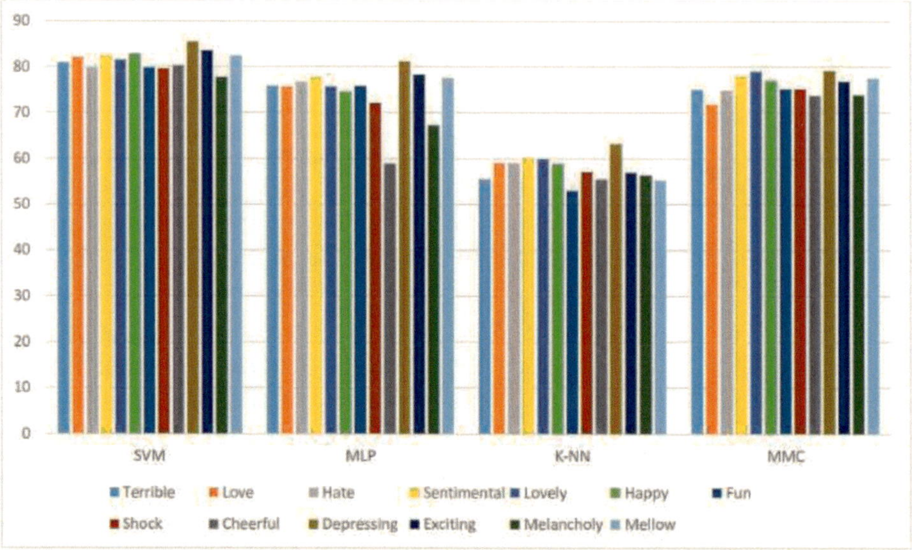

Fig. (9.2). Performance analysis of different classifiers with large number of emotions.

Fig. (**9.2**) shows the results of many classifiers (32 EEG and eight peripheral). As can be seen, compared to the Fig. (**9.2**) fusion results of only 32 EEG channel characteristics, there isn't much of an improvement. It's worth mentioning that the K-NN classifier's classification accuracy has improved. The performance improved with the MLP and MMC classifiers in a few cases, and only one improvement with the SVM classifier in the 'Melancholy' emotion.

The parameter epsilon (ε) determines the width of the margin around the regression curve. The number of support vectors used is influenced by this parameter. As feature vectors outside or close to the margin border are commonly used as support vectors, a larger margin results in fewer support vectors. The number of support vectors is computationally relevant since the summing is reduced to the summation of the support vectors only.

After completing testing on the range [0,1], we decided on ε = 0.001. MLP offers a high level of accuracy when it comes to categorization. Over the 640 training instances, a tenfold cross-validation test is used to classify each classifier.

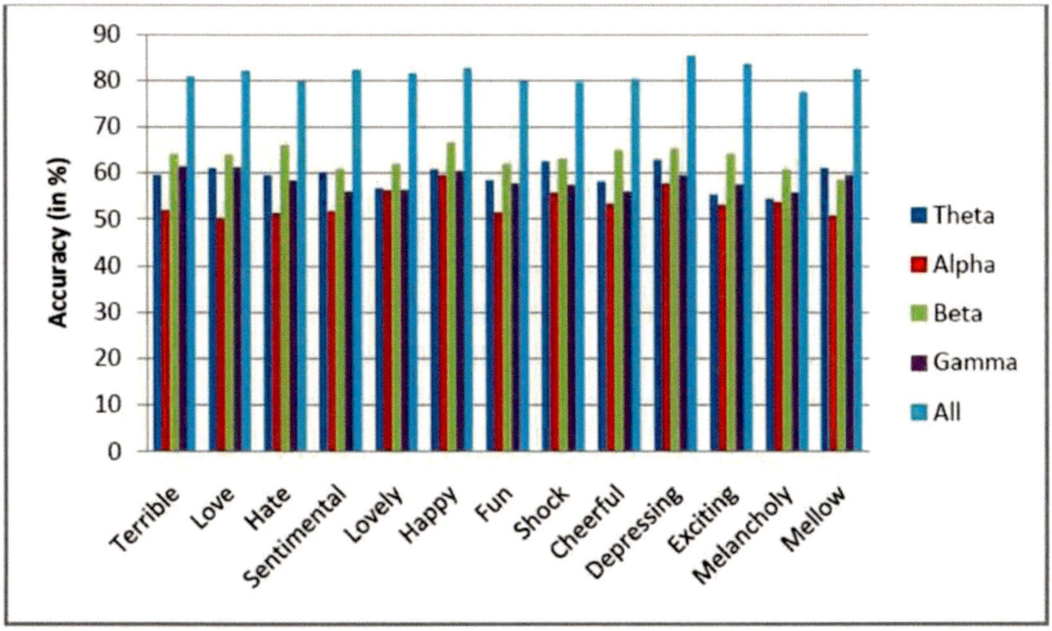

Fig. (9.3). Performance with SVM classifier for different emotions with the EEG frequency band; 'All' represents all bands.

Fig. (**9.3**). demonstrates that feature fusion, which combines multiple frequency characteristics, outperforms each band. As a result, the fusion in our suggested technique occurs at two levels: one at distinct frequency band characteristics and the other at varied channel features. The other modalities appear to function in concert with one another. Collecting emotional data is a time-consuming process complicated by subject physiological variations, signal-to-noise ratios, and the quality of emotion evaluations. Even the feature richness of the EEG signal, which is attributable to its vast frequency bandwidth, may not be present in peripheral signals.

Table **9.1** depicts the comparative performance with similar studies. K. Schaaff *et al.* [16] reported 66.7% accuracy using an SVM classifier with three classes of emotions. The three classes used by K. Schaaff are 1) pleasant, 2) neutral, and 3) unpleasant. They employed STFT to extract features from the EEG data. Our findings suggest that, when it comes to emotion identification from physiological data, the DWT outperforms the STFT. M. Soleymani *et al.* [11] study a success rate of 68.50 percent. With an average success rate of 81.45 percent, it is apparent that our suggested strategy surpasses others. Some EEG emotion recognition studies only reported results based on valence and arousal measurements, which are not included for comparison in this study.

Table 9.1. Accuracy comparisons of various studies based on EEG signal.

Study	Features	Method / Database	Accuracy (%)
K. Schaaff *et. al.*, 2009 [16]	Alpha frequency, power and cross-correlation features	SVM /EEG data of University of Karlsruhe (TH)	66.70 (3 class)
M. Soleymani *et. al.*, 2011 [11]	GSR, EEG, Respiration pattern, Skin temperature	HMM / MAHNOB-HCI	68.50 (9 class)
Atkinson, John, and Daniel Campos, 2016 [17]	mRMR-based	SVM/ DEAP	A/V: 73.06/73.14
Tong *et al* ., 2018 [18]	Logistic regression algorithm	Adaboost algorithm	68% for arousal & 66% for valence
Li, Yang, *et al* ., 2018 [19]	BiDANN	LSTM+Softmax / SEED	92.38 (3 class)
Puk, Kin Ming, *et al* ., 2019 [20]	ADMM-based	Multi-class SGL /MAHNOB	74
Gao, Zhongke, *et al* ., 2020, [21]	Spatial-temporal	Pooling+Softmax SEED/DEAP	90.63 A/V: 92.92/92.24 (3 class)
This method [2021]	**RPE, LRPE**	SVM, MLP / DEAP	**81.45 (13 class)**

CONCLUSION

This chapter presents a multimodal fusion framework for emotion recognition from physiological signals like EEG and Peripheral. The DEAP, a multimodal database of EEG and peripheral signals with 32 participants, was used for all the experimentation. Power energy features and their derivatives were extracted from all bands of EEG and peripheral data. The classification results show that the above features are useful in detecting emotion. It is also evident that SVM outperformed with 81.45% accuracy compared to an existing system.

REFERENCES

[1] S. Koelstra, A. Yazdani, M. Soleymani, and C. Mü, "Single trial classification of EEG and peripheral physiological signals for recognition of emotions induced by music videos", *Proc. Brain Informatics,* pp. 89-100, 2010.

[2] J. Kim, and E. André, "Emotion recognition based on physiological changes in music listening", *IEEE Trans. Pattern Anal. Mach. Intell.,* vol. 30, no. 12, pp. 2067-2083, 2008. [http://dx.doi.org/10.1109/TPAMI.2008.26] [PMID: 18988943]

[3] P. Ekman, "Facial Expression and Emotion", *American Psychologist,* vol. 384, no. 392, 1993. [http://dx.doi.org/10.1037/0003-066X.48.4.384]

[4] R. A. McFarland, "Relationship of skin temperature changes to the emotions accompanying music", *Applied Psychophysiology and Biofeedback,* vol. 255, no. 267, 1985. [http://dx.doi.org/10.1007/BF00999346]

[5] P. Ekman, R.W. Levenson, and W.V. Friesen, "Autonomic nervous system activity distinguishes among emotions", *Science,* vol. 221, no. 4616, pp. 1208-1210, 1983. [http://dx.doi.org/10.1126/science.6612338] [PMID: 6612338]

[6] J.A. Healey, and R.W. Picard, "Detecting stress during real-world driving tasks using physiological sensors", *IEEE Trans. Intell. Transp. Syst.,* vol. 6, no. 2, pp. 156-166, 2005. [http://dx.doi.org/10.1109/TITS.2005.848368]

[7] M. Pantic, M. Valstar, R. Rademaker, and L. Maat, "Web-based database for facial expression analysis", *Proc. IEEE Int'l Conf. Multimedia and Expo,* 2005pp. 317-321

[8] E. Douglas-Cowie, R. Cowie, I. Sneddon, C. Cox, O. Lowry, M. McRorie, J.C. Martin, L. Devillers, S. Abrilian, A. Batliner, N. Amir, and K. Karpouzis, "The HUMAINE Database: Addressing the collection and annotation of naturalistic and induced emotional data", *Proc. Second Int'l Conf. Affective Computing and Intelligent Interaction,* 2007pp. 488-500 [http://dx.doi.org/10.1007/978-3-540-74889-2_43]

[9] M. Grimm, K. Kroschel, and S. Narayanan, "The Vera am Mittag German audio-visual emotional speech database", *Proc. IEEE Int'l Conf. Multimedia and Expo,* 2008pp. 865-868 [http://dx.doi.org/10.1109/ICME.2008.4607572]

[10] G. McKeown, M.F. Valstar, R. Cowie, and M. Pantic, "The SEMAINE corpus of emotionally colored character interactions", *Proc. IEEE Int'l Conf. Multimedia and Expo,* 2010pp. 1079-1084

[11] M. Soleymani, "A multimodal database for affect recognition and implicit tagging", *IEEE Tran. On Affective Computing,* vol. 3, no. 1, 2012. a

[12] S. Koelstra, C. Muhl, M. Soleymani, Jong-Seok Lee, A. Yazdani, T. Ebrahimi, T. Pun, A. Nijholt, and I. Patras, "DEAP: A database for emotion analysis; using physiological signals", *IEEE Trans. Affect. Comput.,* vol. 3, no. 1, pp. 18-31, 2012. [http://dx.doi.org/10.1109/T-AFFC.2011.15]

[13] C. Stickel, J. Fink, and A. Holzinger, "Enhancing Universal Access – EEG Based Learnability Assessment", *Lect. Notes Comput. Sci.,* vol. 4556, pp. 813-822, 2007. [http://dx.doi.org/10.1007/978-3-540-73283-9_88]

[14] F. Karray, M. Alemzadeh, A. Saleh, and M. Nours, "Human-Computer Interaction: An Overview", *Int. Jour. on smart sensing and intelligent systems,* vol. 1, no. 1, 2008.

[15] "Weka machine learning tool", Available from: http://www.cs.waikato.ac.nz/ml/weka/downloading.html

[16] K. Schaaff, and T. Schultz, "Towards emotion recognition from electroencephalography signals", *3rd International Conference on Affective Computing and Intelligent Interaction,* 2009 Amsterdam NL

[17] J. Atkinson, and D. Campos, "Improving BCI-based emotion recognition by combining EEG feature selection and kernel classifiers", *Expert Syst. Appl.,* vol. 47, pp. 35-41, 2016. [http://dx.doi.org/10.1016/j.eswa.2015.10.049]

[18] Z. Tong, "Emotion recognition based on photoplethysmogram and electroencephalogram", *2018 IEEE 42nd annual computer software and applications conference (COMPSAC).,* vol. 2, 2018 [http://dx.doi.org/10.1109/COMPSAC.2018.10266]

[19] Y. Li, W. Zheng, Z. Cui, T. Zhang, and Y. Zong, "A Novel Neural Network Model based on Cerebral Hemispheric Asymmetry for EEG Emotion Recognition", *IJCAI (U. S.),* pp. 1561-1567, 2018. [http://dx.doi.org/10.24963/ijcai.2018/216]

[20] K.M. Puk, "Emotion recognition and analysis using ADMM-based sparse group lasso", *IEEE Trans. Affect. Comput.,* 2019.

[21] Z. Gao, "A channel-fused dense convolutional network for EEG-based emotion recognition", *IEEE Trans. Cogn. Dev. Syst.,* 2020.

CHAPTER 10

Emotions Modelling in 3D Space

Abstract: In this study, we have discussed emotion representation in two and three-dimensional space. The three-dimensional space is based on the three emotion primitives, *i.e.*, valence, arousal, and dominance. The multimodal cues used in this study are EEG, Physiological signals, and video (under limitations). Due to the limited emotional content in videos from the DEAP database, we have considered only three classes of emotions, *i.e.*, happy, sad, and terrible. The wavelet transforms, a classical transform, were employed for multi-resolution analysis of signals to extract features. We have evaluated the proposed emotion model with standard multimodal datasets, DEAP. The experimental results show that SVM and MLP can predict emotions in single and multimodal cues.

Keywords: Arousal, DEAP database, Dominance, EEG, Multiresolution analysis, Support vector machine, Valence.

10.1. INTRODUCTION

Emotion modelling is an effective mechanism to implement emotions in various domains like Artificial Intelligence, Robotics, Psychology and Human-Computer Interaction. Modelling emotions enables machines to exhibit human being like behavior. With the advancement of technology, affect recognition is shifting from distinct emotions toward continuous two or three-dimensional space. Now, researchers focus on the investigation of the dimensional model of emotion. The Dimensional model deals with complex emotions that can be represented by two or three-dimension space. Generally, a 2D model has two dimensions: valence and arousal (in positive and negative axes). A 2D model is typically represented by four quadrants. Some scholars have used various terminologies for distinct emotion dimensions.

Whissell [1] developed a two-dimensional emotion model based on appraisal and activation. We looked at some studies on emotion representation in two-dimensional spaces. We reviewed the two-dimensional emotion model in this chapter. The limitations of the two-dimensional model and the needs of the three-dimensional emotion model are discussed. We will examine how emotions are represented in three-dimensional VAD spaces. After that, a 3D emotion graph is

Gyanendra K. Verma

presented by expressing many emotions in three-dimensional space. In separate portions of this chapter, emotion predictions from multimodal signals are also defined. Finally, we conclude this chapter by presenting the essential findings and contributions.

To represent emotions in three-dimensional space, we used the DEAP database [2], an extensive database encompassing more than twenty-five emotions [3, 4, 5] have all effectively employed the DEAP database in emotion recognition experiments.

The significant contributions of this work for predicting multimodal emotion in VAD space are as follows:

1. It presents the approach for affect prediction regarding valence, arousal, and dominance based on facial expression, EEG, and peripheral cues.
2. It also predicts the correlation between emotion dimensions and demonstrates significant performance improvement.
3. It compares state-of-the-art machine learning techniques *i.e.*, Support Vector Machine and Multilayer Perceptron for continuous affect prediction.

10.2. AFFECT REPRESENTATION IN 2D SPACE

Whissell [1] proposed a two-dimensional emotion model based on the appraisal and activation of two values. They depict the location of emotive words in a (-3; +3) Evaluation-Activation (EA) space. Each of the six Ekman's fundamental emotions is represented as a 2D EA space. Each emotion has specific affective weights to be determined by the emotion analyzer.

Fig. (**10.1**) illustrates the 2D valence-arousal space as proposed by Whissell. It is fascinating that the emotion of 'joy' exists in isolation, even though it should be associated with cheerfulness and pleasure. Furthermore, the emotions' surprise' and 'joy' belong to the same quadrant 2. Furthermore, intermediary states between 'joy' and the rest of the emotions are rarely detected by the Whissell space. As a result, we may conclude that the existing theory cannot be validated using this two- dimensional model. Now the open question is whether two-dimension space suffices to represent all emotions or if there is a need for more dimensions to represent emotions efficiently.

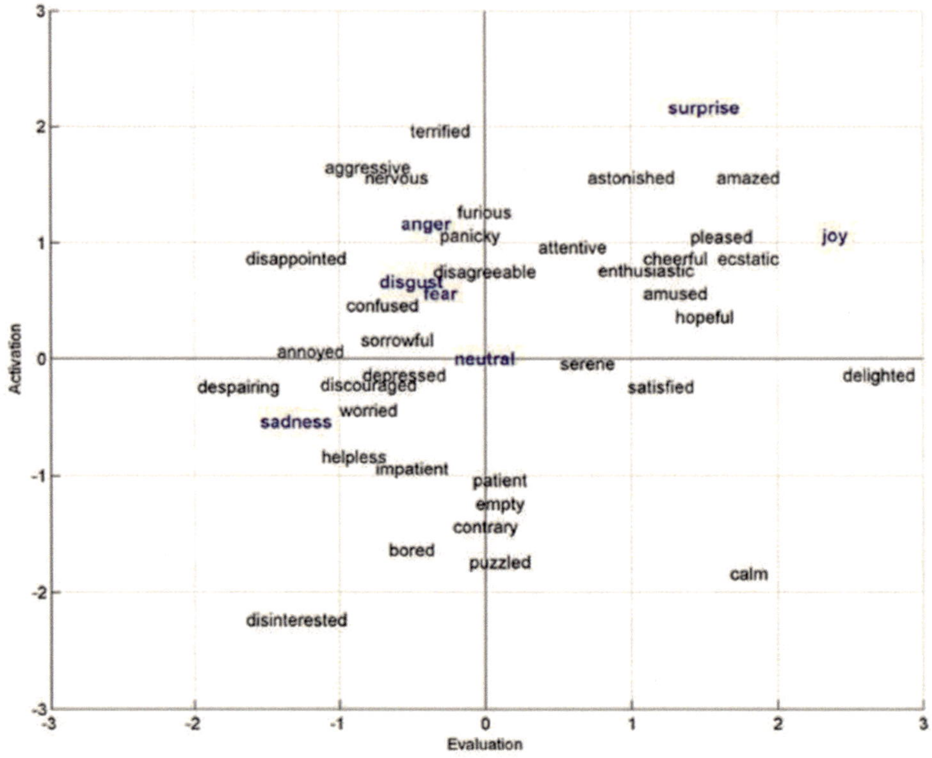

Fig (10.1). EV space as proposed by Whissell.

In an article [6], an anonymous researcher described a mood and emotion monitoring experiment. The resultant map of emotions shows that the two-dimensional mood measure does an excellent job of capturing emotional states. The positive and powerful feelings, such as pride, excitement, and joy, ended up in the space's top right quadrant. Irritation, anguish, and worry were in the third quadrant, which was the reverse of the first. The weak emotions are around the center of the arousal scale. However, stronger emotions are in the higher and lower regions of the plane, depending on valence.

As can be seen from Fig. (**10.2**), 'contentment,' 'affection,' and 'sadness,' are in the same valence axis in the VA space, which is not feasible according to existing theory. However, because the feeling 'affection' lies in the cheerful group, it must be close to the word 'joy.' This model also incorporates restricted emotions.

In valence-arousal space, this model is unable to reflect emotions appropriately. So, once again, the issue arises: do we need more dimensions to express emotions correctly?

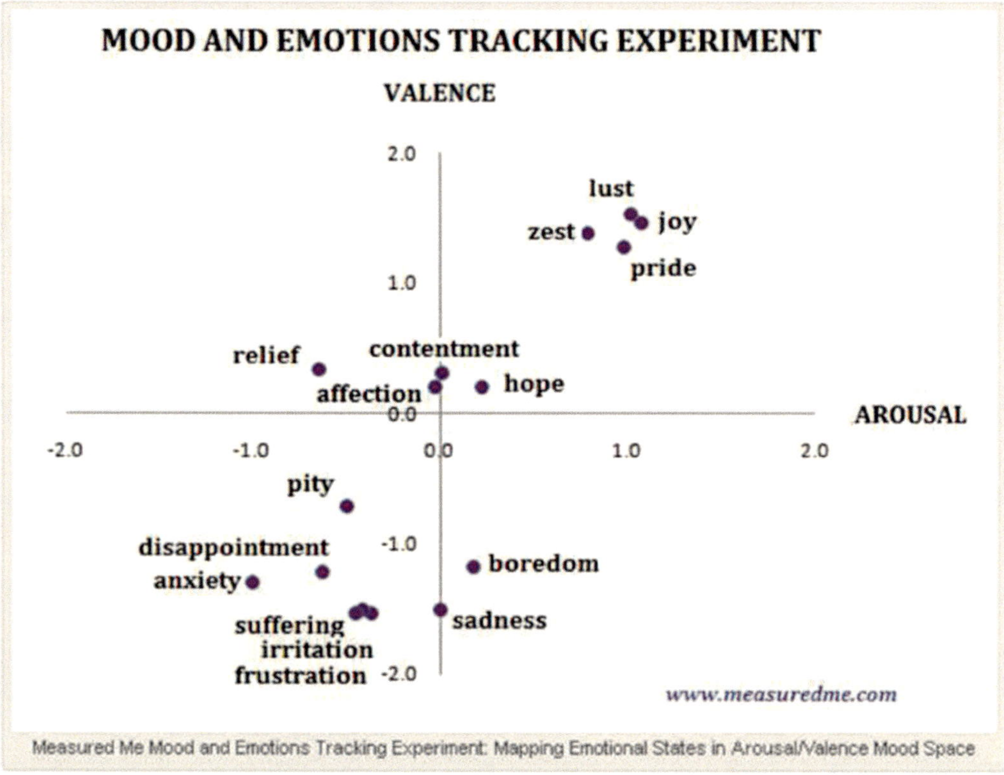

Fig (10.2). mapping mood and emotions in valence/arousal [6].

It is evident from the previous two research experiments that 2D space does not suffice to represent all emotions. Also, the validation is not proper. As a result, we have chosen to investigate the three-dimensional representation of emotions.

10.3. EMOTION REPRESENTATION IN 3D SPACE

Valence, Arousal, and Dominance are the three emotion dimensions in the 3D emotion paradigm.

- **Valence:** On a scale of one to ten, valence runs from unpleasant to please to joyous.
- **Arousal:** Arousal is a scale that spans from calm to aroused to excited.
- **Dominance:** There are five levels of dominance, ranging from submissive (or "without control") to dominant (or "in charge, empowered").

Likeability and familiarity are two further attributes that are not considered because they are insignificant for detecting emotions. Based on these assumptions, we suggested a 3D emotion model in continuous VAD space.

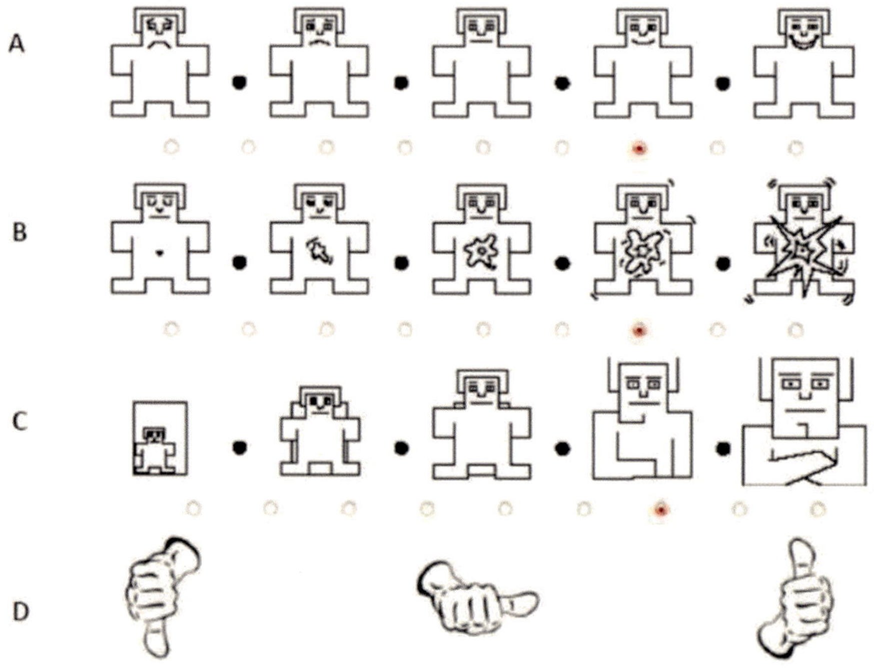

Fig (10.3). SAM method to measure VAD values with liking [7].

Thirty-two patients' EEG and peripheral physiological data were collected while watching a one-minute clip from 40 music video clips. Participants next judged the emotional state caused by each movie using the Self-Assessment Manikins (SAM) scales [7], a method of self-assessment of emotional states, as shown in Fig. (**10.3**). Excitation, arousal, and pleasure intensity scales are represented graphically with nine levels ranging from 1 to 9 that describe their emotional state in terms of four levels: valence, arousal, dominance, and liking. The liking scale was represented by a thumbs up/thumbs down gesture.

According to Schuller B [8], estimating emotion on a continuous-valued scale is a crucial alternative to emotion categories for the computing community to explain human emotional experiences.

10.4. 3D EMOTION MODELING VAD SPACE

We propose a three-dimensional emotion model based on three emotion dimensions (valence, arousal, and dominance) based on the evaluation of a large number of emotions (fun, happy, joy, cheerful, melancholy, depressing, terrible, exciting, love, lovely, sentimental, sad, mellow, shock, hate, *etc.*). The DEAP database, which was used in this study, contains a wide range of emotions. There is no prior knowledge about their VAD placements in three dimensions. The region in the VAD space where each emotion may be regarded to be appropriately positioned in VAD space must be defined in order to assess the model. As shown in Fig. (**10.4**), a total of 1280 VAD values (40 trials for every 32 items) are represented in 3D space for this purpose.

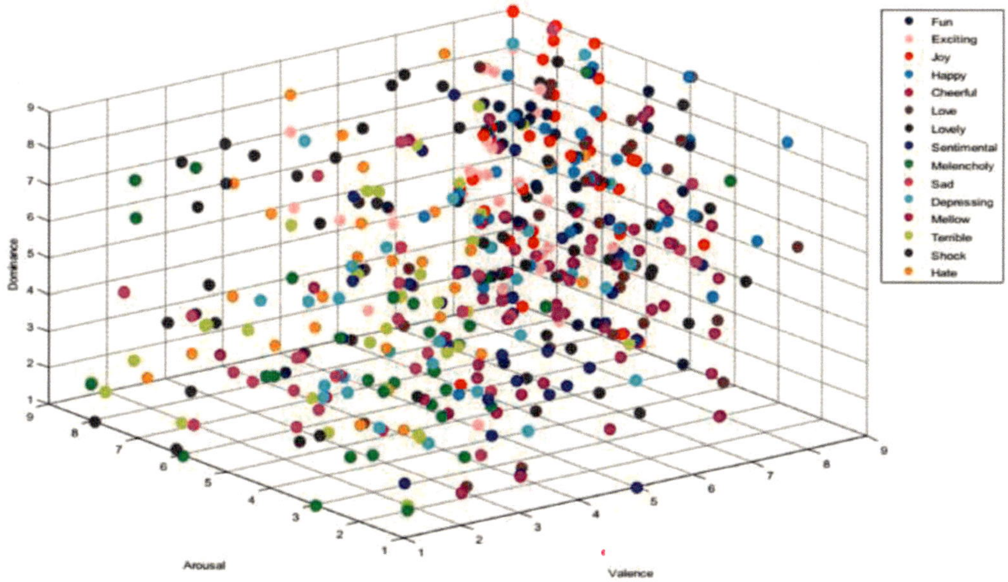

Fig. (10.4). various emotions in VAD space.

We use K-mean clustering to compute the cluster of a collection of emotions, despite the fact that there are various ways to do it. Some outliers have been deleted; a point has been deemed an outlier if its coordinate value is extremely high or extremely low. The emotion centroid in VAD space, as well as the Euclidean distances between each emotion, were calculated. Table **10.1** shows that the model is valid, with a maximum distance of 4.70 between Happy and Sad and a minimum distance of 0.27 between Fun and Exciting.

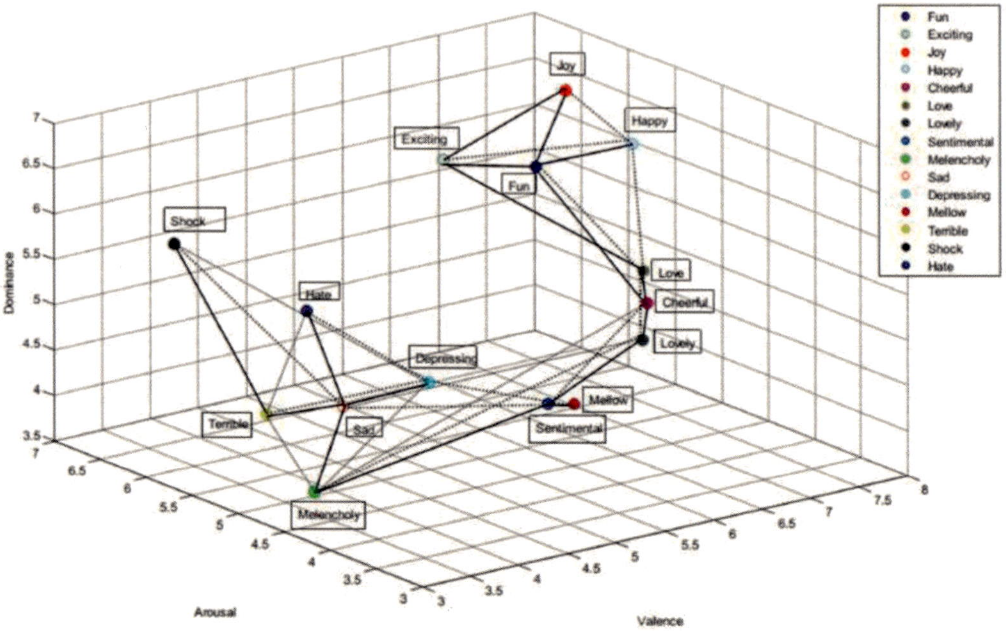

Fig. (10.5). Emotion graph based on the distance among emotions; Solid line – minimum distance | dotted line – 2nd minimum distance | dash line – 3rd minimum distance.

Table 10.1. Euclidean distances of each emotion from other emotions based on centroid in VAD space.

	E1	E2	E3	E4	E5	E6	E7	E8	E9	E10	E11	E12
E1	0	4.7024	2.7903	3.0255	1.1539	1.2791	0.6569	2.0658	1.3311	3.7630	4.1819	2.5741
E2	4.7024	0	2.0866	2.4879	4.3785	4.1845	4.2124	2.9519	3.9027	2.0082	1.4565	2.7661
E3	2.7903	2.0866	0	0.8270	2.4163	2.1952	2.2290	1.6070	2.3260	2.1677	2.2172	1.4238
E4	3.0255	2.4879	0.8270	0	2.6279	2.3719	2.4409	2.1307	2.7152	2.6873	2.7649	1.5790
E5	1.1539	4.3785	2.4163	2.6279	0	0.2699	0.7221	2.3893	2.0717	3.9552	4.2169	2.8017
E6	1.2791	4.1845	2.1952	2.3719	0.2699	0	0.7304	2.2996	2.0712	3.8264	4.0729	2.6373
E7	0.6569	4.2124	2.2290	2.4409	0.7221	0.7304	0	1.8544	1.4175	3.5065	3.8573	2.2583
E8	2.0658	2.9519	1.6070	2.1307	2.3893	2.2996	1.8544	0	0.9643	1.6977	2.1550	1.0230
E9	1.3311	3.9027	2.3260	2.7152	2.0717	2.0712	1.4175	0.9643	0	2.5764	3.0850	1.6562
E10	3.7630	2.0082	2.1677	2.6873	3.9552	3.8264	3.5065	1.6977	2.5764	0	0.6624	1.7175
E11	4.1819	1.4565	2.2172	2.7649	4.2169	4.0729	3.8573	2.1550	3.0850	0.6624	0	2.1546
E12	2.5741	2.7661	1.4238	1.5790	2.8017	2.6373	2.2583	1.0230	1.6562	1.7175	2.1546	0

Note: E1 – happy, E2 – sad, E3 – anger, E4 – hate, E5 – fun, E6 – exciting, E7 – joy, E8 – cheerful, E9 – love, E10 – sentimental, E11 – melancholy, E12 – pleasure.

The number of clusters in Fig. (**10.6**) is the same as the number of emotions in this emotion network (or graph). (Happy, Joy, Fun, Exciting), (Love, Cheerful, Pleasure), (Anger, Hate), (Sad), and (Anger, Hate) are the five clusters on the graph (Melancholy, Sentimental). One or two emotions may have been put in distinct categories since the points in Fig.(**10.5**) clusters had significant differences. The emotion network, on the other hand, matches the 3D VAD model of emotion pretty well. Dotted lines were also utilized to show the relative positions of each emotion category at lengths more than (25 percent of max) and less than (25 percent of maximum) (40 percent of maximum).

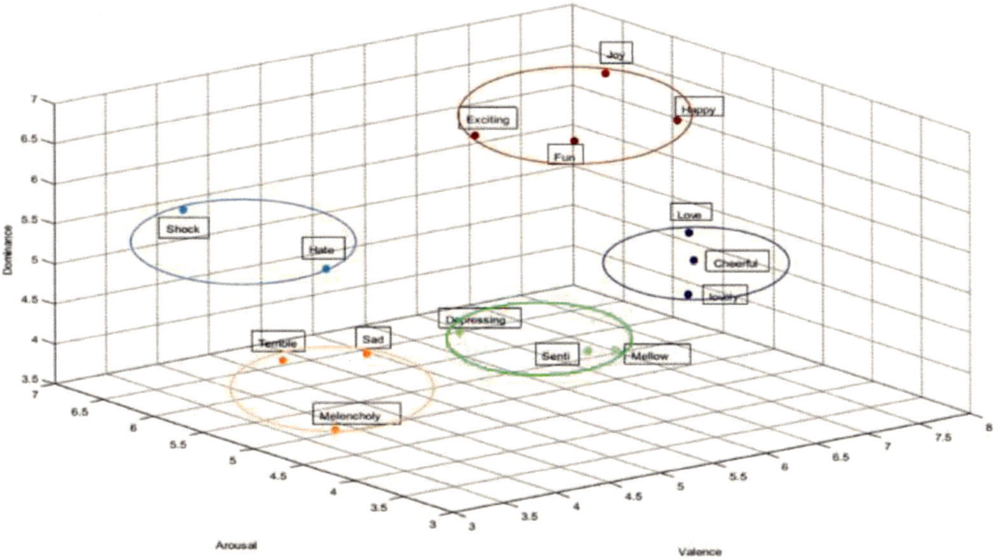

Fig. (10.6). K-mean clustering of emotions.

These findings are consistent with the overall findings. Based on Euclidean distance, we found the closest (1st minimum distance), closer (2nd minimum distance), and near (3rd minimum distance) distance among each of the emotions in another session. Then, in VAD space, all emotions are represented by connecting based on their proximity. A solid line connects emotions that are incredibly close to each other.

The following conclusions may be drawn from the emotion graph shown in Figs. (**10.5** and **10.6**).

- Each emotion is a combination of the three dimensions rather than a single feeling; it may be deduced that emotions are better represented in three-dimensional space.
- In the happy group, valence and arousal are rather high (joy, exciting, cheerful, and fun). The sad group (terrible, sad, and gloomy) and the emotional group, on the other hand, have low valence (depressing, sentimental, and mellow). Dominance is almost non-existent in the sad group of emotions.
- Each dimension has a value for a certain emotion; this emotion graph supports the current emotion theory that the joyous group of emotions is distinct from the sad group of emotions.

The data also demonstrate that the three continuous dimensions of Valence, Arousal, and Dominance (although their values) are sufficient.

The preceding data also show that the three continuous dimensions are sufficient. Emotions are responses to the cognitive assessment of the (abnormal) situation, according to the cognitive appraisal theory. Smith, C.A., and colleagues [9] identified eight components of cognitive assessment. Pleasantness, Attentional activity, Control, Certainty, Goal-Path barrier, Legitimacy, Responsibility, and Anticipated effort are among these traits. Many other researchers have not taken into account the Goal-Path obstacle and Legitimacy. However, we are interested in the standard quantities that come from the evaluation rather than the appraisal itself. Valence conveys a sense of direction, as well as a sense of happiness or melancholy (like hue in color representation).

Arousal refers to the degree of intensity or sharpness (attributed to the attentional activity or expected effort). In contrast, dominance refers to the degree of self- or situational control (which may result from control, certainty, and responsibility). As a result, we believe these three continuous dimensions adequately express an emotion individually.

In addition, we have developed a network of emotions with 12 emotions as nodes and distances as edges in Fig. (**10.6**). To begin, we have used a solid line to represent distances up to 25% of the maximum value (4.7/4=1.18). Fig. (**10.7**) depicts an emotion graph that connects several emotions.

10.5. EMOTION PREDICTION IN THE PROPOSED FRAMEWORK

Researchers have recently begun investigating a dimensional model of emotion, in which single-dimensional 2D or 3D feelings may not accurately capture complex emotional states. Various studies on visuals also utilized the dimensional model of emotions [10, 11, 12].

This study employed EEG, peripheral, and visual signals as multimodal cues. GSR, BVP, EOM, and other peripheral cues are examples of peripheral cues. In contrast, visual cues are frontal face video frames received from DEAP database individuals. We retrieved the video frames after picking and dividing the video into three emotion groups (happy, sad, and surprise). Due to a constraint in the emotional content of films in the DEAP database, we only examined three fundamental emotions (Ekman's emotion). The conclusions derived from video data are constrained. 1) The video frames extracted from videos with high emotional content are manually selected. 2) We chose only three emotion categories: joyful, sad, and surprise because these three categories included the most emotional information; and 3) the number of frames is restricted.

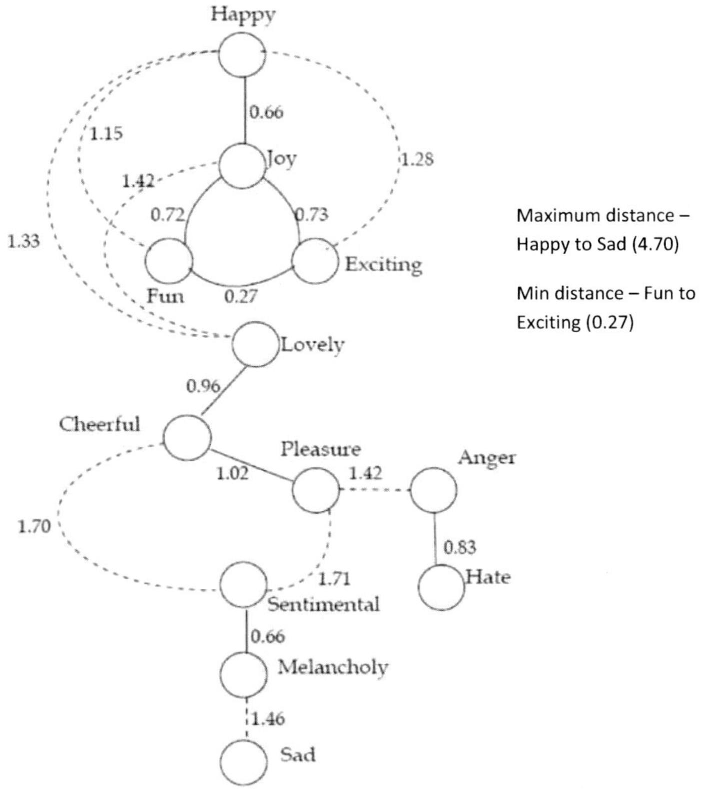

Fig. (10.7). Emotion Graph.

The three phases of the approach are as follows: 1) Data processing in many modes. Fig. (**10.8**) depicts the processing of VAD data and the prediction of emotion. Pre-processing, feature extraction, and feature normalization are part of multimodal data processing. Each modality followed these procedures, including video, EEG, and peripheral cues. For each modality, multiple pre-processing algorithms were used, detailed in their respective area of feature extraction.

10.5.1. Multimodal Data Processing

In the multimodal data processing stage, the pre-segmented video, EEG, and peripheral segments of the DEAP database are used. DWT is applied with the "Daubechies" for feature extraction from face data. Similarly, we applied DWT to capture spontaneous emotion from EEG and peripheral cues. Data processing for VAD entails categorizing input data into three categories: low, medium, and high, for example, low and high arousal. Regarding VAD, we collected ground truth data for each modality.

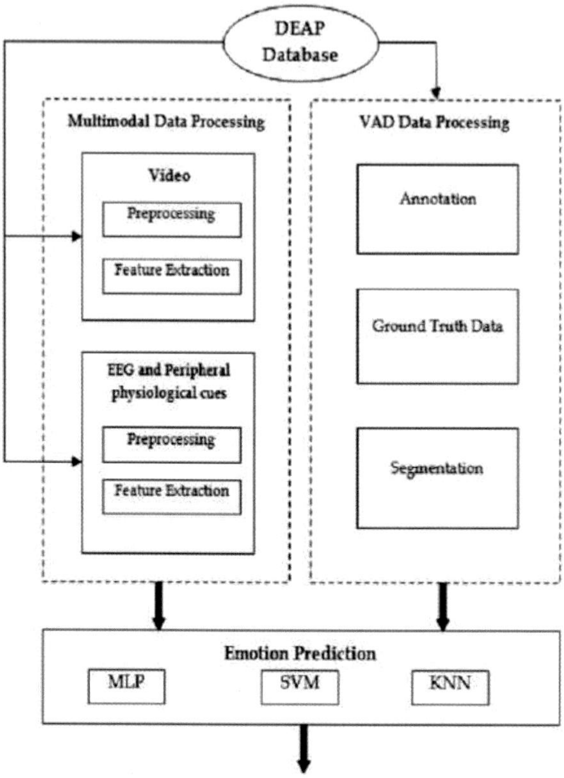

Fig. (10.8). Proposed methodology to predict emotion from multimodal cues.

10.5.1.1. Prediction of Emotion from a Visual Cue

We utilized Viola and Jones' face detection tools based on a cascade classifier. The DEAP dataset comprises the frontal face picture of several persons. However, some additional background items are in the video/image. As a result, we extracted the face using Viola Jones' frontal face detection tools [13].

The retrieved frame is 720×576 pixels in size. Because the emotional content of films in the DEAP collection is limited, we only investigated three emotion categories for affect recognition (happy, sad, and dreadful). The facial expression samples were taken from movies of various persons with much facial emotion. The video was chosen based on the emotional content that we carefully noticed.

We employed wavelet transform and curvelet transforms to assess facial expression using multiresolution analysis (MRA), since these techniques have been effectively used in [14, 15, 16]. The wavelet transform, which uses multiresolution analysis (MRA) to evaluate the signal, can capture the fine details of visual information. The discrete curvelet transform (DCT) is described in our earlier studies [3, 17, 18] is used to execute the curvelet transform technique. The image data of emotion may contain various backgrounds that is irrelevant to emotion identification. Extracting the frontal face from such data is a challenging task. We used the face detection utilities of Viola-Jones [13], which are based on a cascade classifier, to recognize the face from the video frames. Chung and Yoon [23] proposed a weighted log posterior function-based Bayes classifier to classify affective states. They considered three classes of affective states in the valence and arousal dimensions. They reported 66.6% & 66.4% accuracy for the two classes and 53.4% & 51.0% accuracy for the three classes.

10.5.1.2. Prediction of Emotion from Physiological Cue

Physiological cues are essential in determining whether or not a person's behavior or emotional state has changed. Different physiological cues can be used systematically to increase emotion identification accuracy. Picard *et al.* [19] employed Sequential Forward Floating Selection (SFFS), Fisher Projection, and a mix of these methods to analyze GSR, heartbeat, breathing, and ECG physiological data for emotion identification. The hybrid approach was stated to have an overall accuracy of eighty percent. The visual and physiological signals that have been represented in formative cues for automatic, spontaneous affect identification are the subject of this research.

Most emotion theory demonstrates that physiological characteristics have a role in emotion. P. Ekman *et al.* demonstrated the physiological pattern linked with a specific emotion was demonstrated by P. Ekman *et al.* [20]. For feature extraction, two types of data were employed in this study: EEG and peripheral physiological signals. Frequency and amplitude are two parameters that may be used to define EEG. The EEG signal contains the following frequency bands [21].

10.5.2. Ground Truth Data

The ground truth data for each film from the DEAP database was created using the ratings (valence, arousal, and dominance) supplied by each participant individually. These scales' ratings are divided into three categories (low, medium, and high). The cutoff point is in the center of a 9-point continuous scale. After then, a participant's rating was converted into the designated classifications. We categorize these classes using this technique, as given in table 10.2. This approach uses this approach to segment data into low, medium, and high multimodal segments.

Table 10.2. Valence, Arousal and Dominance class.

Valence	Arousal	Dominance
Unpleasant	Calm	Submissive
Neutral	medium aroused	medium dominant
Pleasant	Excited	dominant

10.5.3. Emotion Prediction

In the last stage, the multimodal information must be classified and fused. Support Vector Machines and an Artificial Neural Network have been deployed to classify multimodal information. We have also combined numerous cues and modalities at the feature level before feeding them to the classifiers. A fusion framework was deployed to predict emotion in terms of VAD. Compared to single cue/modality performance, the fusion architecture delivers much better accuracy.

This model is concerned with the optimum integration of multimodal cues (EEG and peripheral data, for example) at the feature level. We looked at many elements of high and low-level fusion in our work. Based on the multiresolution analysis, the model depicts two central fusion techniques: low- and high- and high-level fusion. The feature bins in low-level fusion are derived from the sub-band decomposition of several input modalities. The feature bins above are then merged to create a composite feature vector. We made optimum feature selection over feature bins of diverse modalities in high-level fusion to get robust features. The classification is then applied to each modality, combining the classification results to provide the choice.

10.6. FEATURE SELECTION AND CLASSIFICATION

All of the experiments make use of the DEAP database. The research employed 40 channel EEG signals with 8056 data and 40 trials per subject for 32 people. Multiresolution analysis with wavelet transforms extracts features from many modalities/cues. Specific statistical metrics are utilized to generate feature vectors for each modality. Before categorization, all characteristics were normalized to the range [0, 1]. We also used an automated frame segmentation approach to analyze thirty videos (a total of 30,000 video frames) for three emotion categories.

The multiresolution analysis is deployed to extract features, and the analysis of variance (ANOVA) approach is used to select them. SVM, KNN, and MLP classifiers are used to classify. A multiresolution analysis is used to extract features, and the analysis of variance (ANOVA) approach is used to select them. Three classifiers are used to make the classifications: SVM, KNN, and MLP.

10.7. RESULTS AND DISCUSSIONS

For visual cues, the wavelet decomposition is based on the size of the video frames. In contrast, the frequency of the signals is used for physiological cues. The 5th-level wavelet decomposition of the video cue yields the wavelet coefficients. We divided the physiological data into five levels because the sampling rate was 128 Hz. Different wavelet families employ the discrete wavelet transform technology to obtain approximation and detail coefficients from input physiological data.

For emotion recognition, we used tenfold cross-validation. We use two machine learning techniques for emotion recognition: SVM and MLP. Various factors within these learning approaches are tuned to achieve optimum results. With the RBF kernel, we achieved the most remarkable accuracy for C= 200 and ε= 0.01 in SVM. The MLP network, too, has two hidden layers and a learning rate of 0.5.

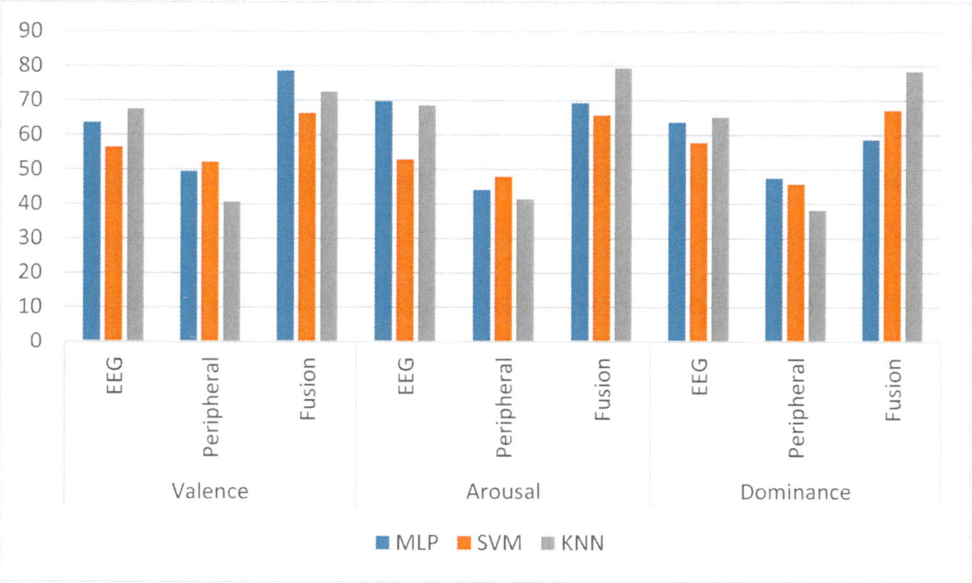

Fig. (10.9). Classification Rate for valence, arousal and dominance with different modalities.

We have done several tests using a single cue, such as EEG, peripheral signals, and their fusion. Fig. (**10.9**, **10.10** and **10.11**) show the performance graph in terms of Classification Rare, F1measure and ROC curve, respectively. For wavelet decomposition, twenty trails of each emotion class were obtained with 32-channel EEG data. As a result, each emotion class has 3220 = 640 samples. 70% of the samples were utilized for training, while the remaining 30% were used for testing. Wavelet analysis was performed using several wavelet families such as db10, coif5, sym10, *etc*. The classification was done using three distinct classifiers: SVM, MLP, and KNN, with the results shown in Figs. (**10.9**, **10.10** and **10.11**).

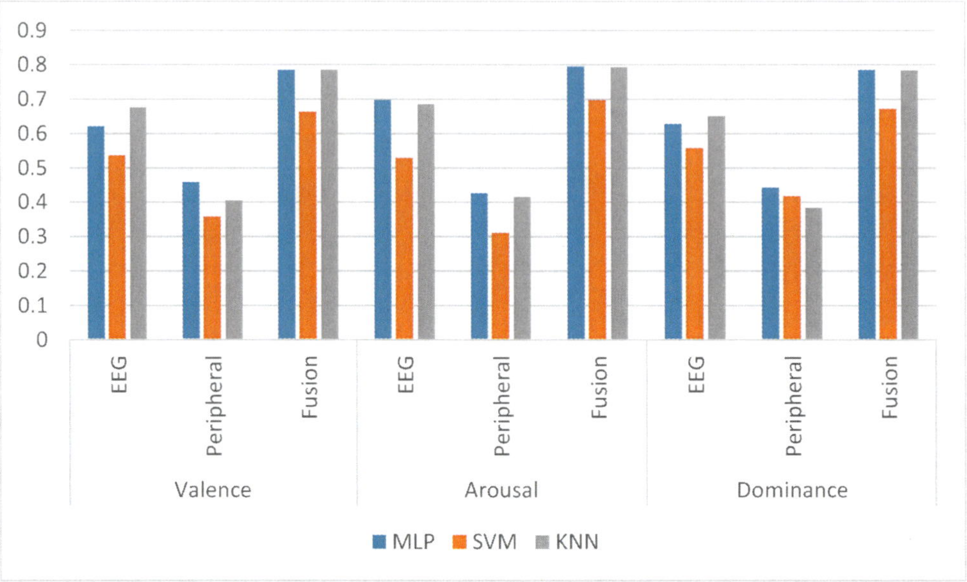

Fig. (10.10). F-1 measures for valence, arousal and dominance with different modalities.

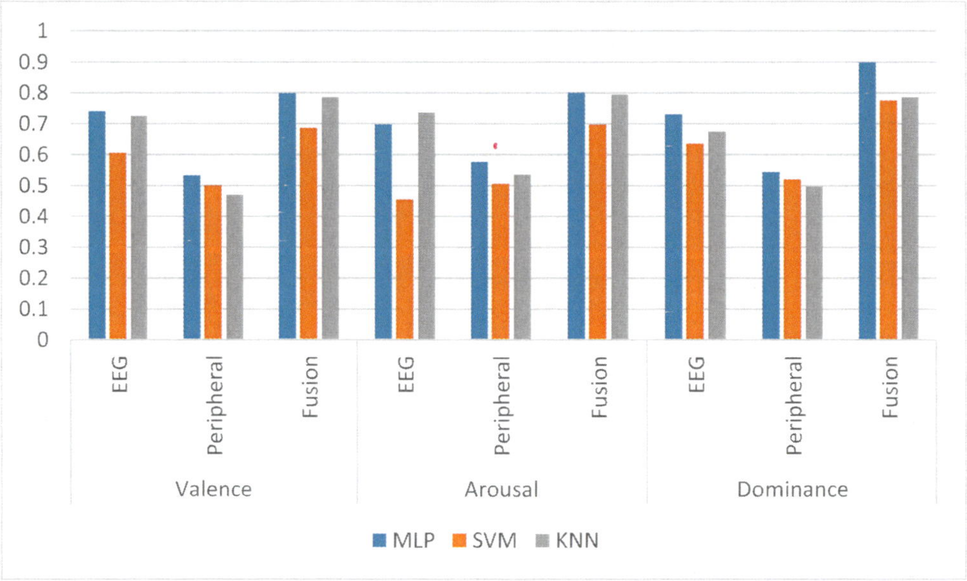

Fig. (10.11). ROC comparison for valence, arousal and dominance with different modalities.

Table 10.3. Confusion Metrics for EEG using MLP (Row: classified Label; Column: Ground Truth) (UnP: Unpleasant | N: Neutral | P: Pleasant) (Calm: Calm| M_Ar: Medium arousal | Exi: Excited) (Sub: Submissive | M_D: Medium dominant | D: Dominant).

-	**UnP**	**N**	**P**
UnP	51.02	46.22	2.743
N	26.41	71.03	2.546
P	38.48	51.25	10.26
Valence			
-	Calm	M_Ar	Exi
Calm	66.55	32.58	0.866
M_Ar	33.35	65.53	1.113
Exi	48.91	34.78	16.30
Arousal			
-	Sub	M_D	D
Sub	65.337	31.214	3.448
M_D	26.840	67.326	5.833
D	35.872	36.588	27.53
Dominance			

Table 10.4. Confusion Metrics for Peripheral using MLP (Row: classified Label; Column: Ground Truth) (UnP: Unpleasant | N: Neutral | P: Pleasant) (Calm: Calm| M_Ar: Medium arousal | Exi: Excited) (Sub: Submissive | M_D: Medium dominant | D: Dominant).

-	**UnP**	**N**	**P**
UnP	99.55	0.321	0.123
N	0.213	99.74	0.037
P	0.555	1.471	97.97
Valence			
-	Calm	M_Ar	Exi
Calm	99.54	0.396	0.059
M_Ar	0.356	99.55	0.089
Exi	1.173	1.434	97.39
Arousal			
-	Sub	M_D	D
Sub	42.43	57.57	1.32
M_D	36.93	63.07	0.625
D	38.39	61.61	0.521

(Table 10.4) cont.....

-	UnP	N	P
Dominance			

The findings in Figs. (**10.9**, **10.10** and **10.11**) are based on a few assessment matrices, such as average accuracy, F-measure, and ROC area. The error rate for different emotion categories produced by MLP is shown in Tables **10.3** and **10.4**. The classification accuracy demonstrates that our strategy performs better than existing studies. However, many EEG emotion recognition results based on valence and arousal measurements are not included in his study for comparison due to the low number of emotions. Fig. (**10.12**) depicts the categorization findings for the three valence, arousal, and dominance classes.

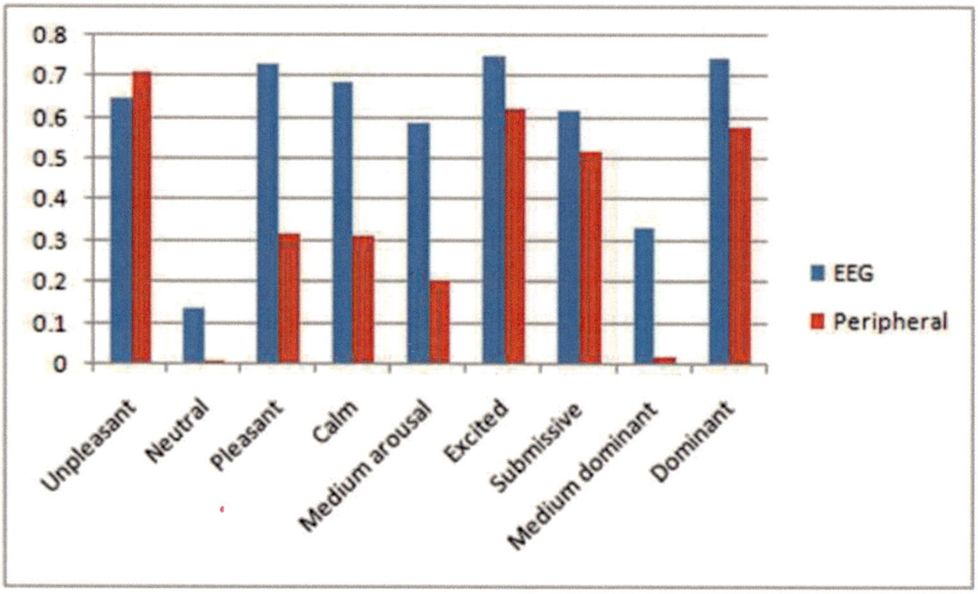

Fig. (10.12). Classification results (using MLP) of each class for different modalities.

Table **10.5** lists prior research that used the DEAP database. Many research use power spectral characteristics to extract features. However, our technique uses MRA, which increased classification accuracy by 12% in valence, arousal, and dominance classes. The most outstanding achievable accuracies utilizing the DEAP database are 55.4% and 55.2% for three classes of valence and arousal. Our method's classification accuracy for valence and arousal is 67.51% and 69.62%, respectively. In addition, compared to other recent research, our suggested technique has improved classification accuracy while requiring less computing effort.

Table 10.5. Comparative performance.

Study	Features	Performance
Koelstra *et al.*, 2012 [2]	Spectral features	57.6%(V) 62.0% (A)
Chung and Yoon *et al.* 2012 [22]	Spectral features and Bays	66.6% (V)*, 53.4% (V)#
Yoon H. J.and Chung S. Y., 2013 [23]	Fast Fourier with Bays	70.9% (V) 70.1%(A)*, 55.4%(V), 55.2% (A)#
Tripathi *et al.* 2017 [24]	Convolutional Neural Network	66.79% (V), 57.58% (A)
Siddharth *et al* . 2019 [25]	VGG-16 Convolutional Neural Network	EEG -61.24%/0.60% (V), 65.15%/0.63% (A) Cardiac- 58.57%/0.59% (V), 61.84%/0.61% (A) GSR-58.98%/0.57% (V), 61.02%/0.59% (A)
Ganapathy *et al.* 2021 [26]	Multiscale Convolutional Neural Network	69.33% (V) and 71.43% (A)
This method [2021]	MRA with SVM	67.51% (V)*, 69.62%(A)*, 63.57% (D)#

* for two class | # for three class

CONCLUSION

In this study, we have investigated emotion representation on a continuous three-dimensional space. The three emotions, primitive's valence, arousal, and dominance, are used to predict emotion in three dimensions. EEG, physiological data, and video are the multimodal cues utilized in this experiment (under limitations). We only investigated three emotional groups, joyful, sad, and awful, because of the minimal emotional content in films from the DEAP collection. Wavelet transformations are used to extract multimodal information from physiological signals. The proposed emotion model was tested on DEAP multimodal dataset. The experimental findings from single and multimodal cue classification using SVM and MLP are highly encouraging. We also want to put these capabilities to the test for real-time emotion identification in order to establish a human-machine interface.

Multimodal emotion representation in 2D and 3D space and emotion prediction in VAD space are the subjects of this research. The topic of predicting spontaneous emotion using EEG and peripheral signals, and a visual cue (with certain limits) has been considered. The performance of two cutting-edge machine learning approaches, Support Vector Machine (SVM) and Multilayer Perceptron (MLP), is also compared. The following are the primary contributions of this study to forecasting multimodal emotion in VAD space.

- It explains how to anticipate emotion in valence, arousal, and dominance using facial expression, EEG, and peripheral signals.
- It also shows a considerable improvement in performance by predicting the association between emotion dimensions.
- It compares state-of-the-art machine learning algorithms for continuous impact prediction (*e.g.*, Support Vector Machine and Multilayer Perceptron).

REFERENCES

[1] C.M. Whissell, *The dictionary of affect in language, emotion: Theory, research and experience.* vol. Vol. 4. Academic Press: New York, 1989.

[2] S. Koelstra, C. Muhl, M. Soleymani, Jong-Seok Lee, A. Yazdani, T. Ebrahimi, T. Pun, A. Nijholt, and I. Patras, "DEAP: A database for emotion analysis; using physiological signals", *IEEE Trans. Affect. Comput.,* vol. 3, no. 1, pp. 18-31, 2012. [http://dx.doi.org/10.1109/T-AFFC.2011.15]

[3] G.K. Verma, and U.S. Tiwary, *"Multimodal fusion framework: A multiresolution approach for emotion classification and recognition from physiological signals", Neuroimage.* Elsevier, 2013.

[4] H. Gunes, and B. Schuller, "Categorical and dimensional affect analysis in continuous input: Current trends and future directions", *Image Vis. Comput.,* vol. 31, no. 2, pp. 120-136, 2013. [http://dx.doi.org/10.1016/j.imavis.2012.06.016]

[5] Y. Liu, and O. Sourina, *Real-time fractal-based valence level recognition from EEG".* vol. Vol. 7848. Transactions on Computational Science XVIII Lecture Notes in Computer Science, 2013, pp. 101-120.

[6] "Emotion Blog", Available from: http://measuredme.com/2013/02/first-results-of-my-mood-and-emotions-tracking-experiment/

[7] J.D. Morris, "SAM: the self-assessment manikin, An efficient cross-cultural measurement of emotion response", *J. Advert. Res.,* vol. 35, no. 8, pp. 63-68, 1995.

[8] B. Schuller, "Recognizing affect from linguistic information in 3D continuous space", *IEEE Trans. Affect. Comput.,* vol. 2, no. 4, pp. 192-205, 2011. [http://dx.doi.org/10.1109/T-AFFC.2011.17]

[9] C.A. Smith, and P.C. Ellsworth, "Patterns of cognitive appraisal in emotion", *J. Pers. Soc. Psychol.,* vol. 48, no. 4, pp. 813-838, 1985. [http://dx.doi.org/10.1037/0022-3514.48.4.813] [PMID: 3886875]

[10] M.A. Nicolaou, H. Gunes, and M. Pantic, "Continuous prediction of spontaneous affect from multiple cues and modalities in valence-arousal space", *IEEE Trans. Affect. Comput.,* vol. 2, no. 2, pp. 92-105, 2011. [http://dx.doi.org/10.1109/T-AFFC.2011.9]

[11] D. Glowinski, A. Camurri, G. Volpe, N. Dael, and K. Scherer, "Technique for automatic emotion recognition by body gesture analysis", *Proc. IEEE CS Conf. Computer Vision and Pattern Recognition Workshops,* 2008pp. 1-6 [http://dx.doi.org/10.1109/CVPRW.2008.4563173]

[12] M. Wollmer, B. Schuller, F. Eyben, and G. Rigoll, "Combining long short-term memory and dynamic bayesian networks for incremental emotion-sensitive artificial listening", *IEEE J. Sel. Top. Signal Process.,* vol. 4, no. 5, pp. 867-881, 2010. [http://dx.doi.org/10.1109/JSTSP.2010.2057200]

[13] P. Viola, "Rapid object detection using a boosted cascade of simple features", *CVPR,* 2001.

[14] A. Saha, and Q.M. Jonathan, "Facial Expression Recognition using Curvelet based local binary patterns", *IEEE International Conference on Acoustics Speech and Signal Processing (ICASSP),*

2010pp. 2470-2473
[http://dx.doi.org/10.1109/ICASSP.2010.5494892]

[15] X. Wu, and J. Zhao, "Curvelet feature extraction for face recognition and facial expression recognition", *Sixth International Conference on Natural Computation (ICNC),* 2010pp. 1212-1216
[http://dx.doi.org/10.1109/ICNC.2010.5583642]

[16] I. Sumana, M. Islam, D.S. Zhang, and G. Lu, "Content Based Image Retrieval Using Curvelet Transform", *Proc. of IEEE International Workshop on Multimedia Signal Processing,* 2008pp. 11-16 Cairns, Queensland, Australia
[http://dx.doi.org/10.1109/MMSP.2008.4665041]

[17] G.K. Verma, "Facial micro-expression recognition using discrete curvelet transform", *2017 Conference on Information and Communication Technology (CICT),* 2017
[http://dx.doi.org/10.1109/INFOCOMTECH.2017.8340637]

[18] G. Verma, *K2, "Multi-algorithm fusion for speech emotion recognition", ACC-2011, Part III, CCIS 192.* Springer, 2011, pp. 452-459. a

[19] R.W. Picard, E. Vyzas, and J. Healey, "Toward machine emotional intelligence: analysis of affective physiological state", *IEEE Trans. Pattern Anal. Mach. Intell.,* vol. 23, no. 10, pp. 1175-1191, 2001.
[http://dx.doi.org/10.1109/34.954607]

[20] P. Ekman, W.V. Friesen, M. O'Sullivan, A. Chan, I. Diacoyanni-Tarlatzis, K. Heider, R. Krause, W.A. LeCompte, T. Pitcairn, P.E. Ricci-Bitti, K. Scherer, M. Tomita, and A. Tzavaras, "Universals and cultural differences in the judgments of facial expressions of emotion", *J. Pers. Soc. Psychol.,* vol. 53, no. 4, pp. 712-717, 1987.
[http://dx.doi.org/10.1037/0022-3514.53.4.712] [PMID: 3681648]

[21] C. Stickel, J. Fink, and A. Holzinger, "Enhancing Universal Access – EEG Based Learnability Assessment", *Lect. Notes Comput. Sci.,* vol. 4556, pp. 813-822, 2007.
[http://dx.doi.org/10.1007/978-3-540-73283-9_88]

[22] S.Y. Chung, and H.J. Yoon, "Affective classification using Bayesian classifier and supervised learning", *12th International Conference on Control, Automation and System (ICCAS),* 2012pp. 1768-1771

[23] H. J. Yoon, and S. Y. Chung, "EEG-based emotion estimation using Bayesian weighted-log-posterior function and perceptron convergence algorithm", *Computer Biol Med.,* vol. 43, pp. 2230-7, 2013.
[http://dx.doi.org/10.1016/j.compbiomed.2013.10.017]

[24] S. Tripathi, S. Acharya, and R.D. Sharma, "Using deep and convolutional neural networks for accurate emotion classification on deap dataset", *Twenty-ninth IAAI conference,* 2017

[25] S. Siddharth, T-P. Jung, and T.J. Sejnowski, "Utilizing deep learning towards multi-modal bio-sensing and vision-based affective computing", *IEEE Trans. Affect. Comput.,* 2019.

[26] N. Ganapathy, Y.R. Veeranki, H. Kumar, and R. Swaminathan, "Emotion recognition using electrodermal activity signals and multiscale deep convolutional neural network", *J. Med. Syst.,* vol. 45, no. 4, p. 49, 2021.
[http://dx.doi.org/10.1007/s10916-020-01676-6] [PMID: 33660087]

SUBJECT INDEX

A

B

C

D

E

F

G

H

I

K

L

M

N

O

P

R

S

Made in the USA
Las Vegas, NV
13 November 2024

40539c75-9d83-42fa-b37b-290f5960545eR01